Mitla Zapotec Texts

Summer Institute of Linguistics
Language Data Amerindian Series

Publication 12

Folklore Texts in Mexican
Indian Languages 3

Nadine Rupp
Series Editor

Mitla Zapotec Texts

Morris Stubblefield and Carol Stubblefield

Compilers

Jerónimo Quero
Pedro Aguilar
Manuel Quero Olivero
Fausto Sosa

Narrators

A Publication of
The Summer Institute of Linguistics
Dallas
1994

LANGUAGE DATA is a serial publication of the Summer Institute of Linguistics, Inc. The series is intended as an outlet for data-oriented papers authored by members of the Institute. All volumes are issued as microfiche editions, while certain selected volumes are also printed in off-set editions.

Copies of this and other publications of the Summer Institute of Linguistics may be obtained from

International Academic Bookstore
7500 W. Camp Wisdom Road
Dallas, TX 75236

Contents

Editor's Preface vii

Introduction 1

The First Man, Woman, and Children 5
    Jerónimo Quero

John the Charcoal Maker 41
    Jerónimo Quero

The Rabbit and the Coyote 61
    Pedro Aguilar

The Lion Meets a Man 103
    Pedro Aguilar

The Man Who Went to Town 123
    Manuel Quero Olivero

A Person of the Earth Who Was Cold All the Time 129
    Manuel Quero Olivero

The Turtle and the Buzzard 135
    Fausto Sosa

The Smallest Animal 143
    Manuel Quero Olivero

Editor's Preface

This is the third volume in the series "Folklore Texts in Mexican Indian Languages" published by the Summer Institute of Linguistics. The texts are accompanied by a short cultural sketch, a brief description of the phonemes, and information on the narrators.

The publication of texts in this series combines the results of linguistic and anthropological research sponsored by the Summer Institute of Linguistics and makes available to the general public some valuable cultural material.

The literal translation lines of the texts present the closest English equivalents of each Zapotec word. When a Zapotec word contains more than one morpheme, the English equivalents of each morpheme are given in the same order, separated by hyphens. When the English equivalent of a Zapotec word or morpheme requires more than one word, these are separated by carets. QM indicates a question marker. The free translation lines present close approximations of the content of each Zapotec sentence in natural English and Spanish. Implicit information is enclosed in parenthesis and Spanish loan words are enclosed in wedges < >.

This volume of Mitla Zapotec texts covers a variety of subjects. The first one is an account of "firsts"; the first corn, the first tortillas, the first tools, the first man and woman, and the first children. The term 'real-god' is used as well as a word referring to the liar. Perhaps these are references to the supreme God and the highest Evil. The first boy and girl meet the real-god and are told that the boy is destined to become the sun and the girl the moon.

"Juan the Charcoal Man" is a story of a man and his donkey and their business dealings. "The Rabbit and The Coyote" relates the woes of the coyote as he is tricked again and again by the smaller rabbit. "The Lion and the Man" tells of how man domesticated the ox, the donkey and the horse, but the man and the lion agree to leave one another alone.

In "The Farmer" the dog is scared to the point that he begins to talk. In "The Person Who was Cold All the Time," a man dies and goes to heaven. Since he was very cold, arrangements are made for him to go to the other side until he warms up. "The Smallest Animal," one that can't be seen, is described as one that lives on the head of a flea. In "The Buzzard and the Turtle" story, the turtle tricks the buzzard into transporting him some distance on his back to find water. The turtle continually tries to distract the buzzard from his intention to eat the turtle.

The compilers of these stories, Morris and Carol Stubblefield, began field work in the Mitla Zapotec language in 1966.

Nadine Rupp
Editor

Introduction

Cultural Sketch of Mitla Zapotec

The Mitla Zapotec live in and near the cultural center of San Pablo Villa de Mitla in the eastern part of the District of Tlacolula, Oaxaca, Mexico. Mitla is located twenty-five miles southeast of Oaxaca City just off the Pan-American highway. The altitude ranges from 5,600 feet in Mitla to 7,500 in Santo Tomas de Arriba to less than 3,000 in other Zapotec towns. There are approximately 18,000 speakers of this Zapotec language in eight towns. Some variations of the language exist from town to town but each understands and is understood by all others. In Mitla, as late as 1970, the /g/ and /y/ were in contrast in identical environments in some words but in free variation in other words. One knows from which side of town another comes by their use of the /g/ and /y/.

The economy for much of the area is based largely on subsistence agriculture with principal crops of corn, beans, and squash. The lower elevation towns grow bananas, coconuts, mameys, custard apples, limes, oranges, sapotes, and other fruit. Mitla's economy is now based largely on tourist trade and trucking. Before there were roads in the area the men traveled by mule east to the Mixe Indians, north to other Zapotec areas, and further north to the Chinantec areas. They transported items for sale and bought coffee and avocados to sell on their return trip. Roads now exist throughout that area. Some Mitlenos have sold their mules, purchased trucks and moved their families into those areas to open stores and act as brokers in buying and selling produce. It was during the time of

1

travel with mules and donkeys that the men would tell stories around the campfires at night. Some of them became excellent story tellers.

Approximately fifty years ago the Mitla ruins were opened to the public and have become a popular tourist attraction. Available at this site are many beautiful weavings, rugs, sweaters, items of onyx, crocheted tablecloths, blouses, and bedspreads, clothing, and other items for sale. Many of these articles are made locally while some are purchased from as far away as Guatemala. Some of the onyx is mined nearby and sent to a factory in the state of Puebla to be worked into bowls, lamps, candlesticks, bookends, etc. These are also available for purchase at the market near the ruins.

Pre-conquest Mitla was a town where priests lived. Many folks believe that the spirits of the departed dead come to live in Mitla and it has become known as the "town of the dead." People from other Indian groups still come many miles to buy fruit and bread for All Saints' holidays at the end of October and the first of November. They can get it blessed by the resident priest there.

Education has become very important to the Zapotecs. There are three large primary schools in Mitla and one secondary school. All of the other towns have primary schools. A number of Mitla Zapotecs have graduated from universities with degrees in law, medicine, dentistry, agriculture, and government.

Their artistic ability is evident in the way many can play musical instruments with little or no instruction. Those who are weavers can copy patterns for clothing by looking at pictures or another item of clothing. They use large wooden looms that require the use of both hands and both feet. A few use the waist loom to make smaller articles of clothing, and wall hangings. They make intricate designs on cloth, using either a treadle or electric sewing machine, by leaving off the pressure foot and controlling the design by moving the fabric back and forth by hand.

Brief Description of Mitla Zapotec Phonemes

Consonants. Most Mitla Zapotec consonants are either fortis or lenis. The fortis consonants are: stops *p, t, k, kw*; affricates *ȼ, č*; sibilants *s, š*; nasals *m̲, n̲*; lateral *l̲*; and retroflex *r̲*. The lenis are: stops *b, d, g, gw*; affricates *ǰ, ẓ*; sibilants *z, ž*; nasals *m, n*; lateral *l*; and retroflex *r*. Only the fricatives *f, h* and the semivowels *w, y* are neither fortis nor lenis.

Fortis consonants are pronounced with more strength and are usually longer than lenis consonants. Fortis stops, affricates, and sibilants are all voiceless, but fortis nasals and the fortis lateral are voiced except after an aspirated vowel at the end of root words. The fortis retroflex is also voiced except before another fortis consonant at the beginning of root words.

Lenis consonants are pronounced with less strength than fortis consonants, and they often cause the preceding vowel to lengthen. All lenis consonants are voiced except following an aspirated vowel at the end of root words; this devoicing is written as capitalization.

Vowels. The Mitla Zapotec vowels are *a, ä* [æ], *e, i, o, u;* these all can occur in one of six forms: simple, shortened, lengthened, laryngealized, glottalized, or aspirated.

Simple vowels at the end of root words are shortened before a fortis consonant and lengthened before a lenis consonant or in an open syllable, although these modifications are not written. Laryngealized vowels are written double, glottalized vowels are followed by *?,* and aspirated vowels are followed by *h.*

Suprasegmentals. The final syllable of each root word is stressed and carries high tone. However, neither stress nor tone is written.

Notes on Narrators

The interests of each of the four narrators whose stories occur in this volume is reflected in the type of story they tell. Jerónimo Quero drew from his extensive experiences as he traveled with his mules and donkeys. The first story, "The First Man, Woman, and Children" was recorded in 1966 when he was approximately forty-five years old. It was published in Zapotec and also published in English in "Tlalocan" Volume VI, Number 1, La Casa de Tlaloc, Mexico, DF, 1969. Jeronimo also related the story of "Juan the Charcoal Maker."

Pedro Aguilar is a noted story teller in the town. He told stories to his children and neighboring children as he stood weaving on his hand or waist loom. "The Rabbit and the Coyote" and "The Lion Meets a Man" were told in 1966 when Pedro was forty-five to fifty years of age. Little or no editing has been done on these stories.

Manuel Quero Olivero's stories all seem to be a type of joke with a punch line. "The Man Who Went to Town" and "The Smallest Animal" were told in 1966 when he was twenty years old. "The Person of the Earth Who was Cold All the Time" was recorded in 1979. Parts of these stories have been edited.

Fausto Sosa told "The Turtle and the Buzzard" in 1979 when he was approximately forty years old. This story has been edited extensively.

The First Man, Woman, and Children

Jerónimo Quero

1. *gukwadyahGtu   škwent   Susläiire   nähza   Golgisah ni*
   will-nail-ear-you of-story Susläii-this with-also Golgisah that

   guhk behN̲   ganid šten gejlyuh
   was person first of   town-earth

2. *Golgisahre   gideb ǰeh nagasahni   ro?   te   biliää*
   Golgisah-this all   day is-lying-back-his mouth one cave

1. You listen to the story of this woman, Susläii and Golguisaj, who were the first people in the world.

2. This Golguisaj spent all his time lying in the entrance of a cave.

1. Van ustedes a escuchar el cuento de Susläii y Golguisaj, quienes vivieron al principio del mundo.

2. Golguisaj siempre estaba acostado enfrente de una cueva.

3. *sas   Susläiire   kadeddušni   trabahW risaʔnni   ši*
   and Susläii-this passing-very-she suffering go-leaving-she what

   rahW Golgisahre   siʔkti   ¢uʔn   wält   rwii ši   rahW
   eating Golgisah-this like-just thirteen times see what eating

   Golgisahre   tebjeh
   Golgisah-this one-day

4. *Susläiire   bijäl   lahZni   žo   guhY   žobniil*
   Susläii-this found   heart-his how cooked corn-cooked

5. *Luš lagahk laani runčeeni   šahBni   runčeeni*
   and herself she   be-making-she clothes-her be-making-she

   šsindoorni runčeeni   giraʔti ni   rikiinni
   of-belt-her be-making-she all-just that going-necessary-she

6. *te   jehti   sääreni   roʔ   nisdoo   giropreni*
   one day-just going-they   mouth water-big   two-they

7. *če   bawii Golgisahre   syääd   te   kah lo nisdoo*
   when saw   Golgisah-this will-come   one box on water-big

3. And Susläii was suffering greatly because she was carrying food to Golguisaj who ate thirteen times a day.

4. This Susläii discovered how to cook corn.

5. After this she discovered how to make clothes, her belts, and everything she needed.

6. One day they both went to the ocean shore.

7. Golguisaj saw a box coming towards them on the ocean.

3. Susläii sufría mucho, porque tenía que ir a llevarle la comida como trece veces al día.

4. Susläii encontró un modo de cocer el maíz.

5. Además, inventó cómo hacer su ropa, tejía sus ceñidores y hacía todo lo que necesitaba.

6. Un día, Susläii y su esposo fueron a dar un paseo a la orilla del mar.

7. De pronto Golguisaj vio una caja que venía sobre las aguas del mar.

8. *ǰehk biriini   Susläii rähpni   Te kah syääd   lo*
   then came^out-it Susläii saying-he one box coming-come on

   nisdoo
   water-big

9. *ǰehkti   rähpni   wilääni don   ši   yuʔ nen cahga*
   then-just saying-he took-it let's-see what is in box-that

10. *če   birii   kahre   lo   nisdoore   bawiireni syääd*
    when came^out box-this on water-big-this saw-they will-come

    tyoʔp byuux nenga
    two   child in-that

11. *ǰehk rähpni   tyoʔp byuux syääd   nen ree   rähpni*
    then saying-he two   child will-come in here saying-he

12. *ǰehk bibalazdušreni   saʔksi   nahkreni benšadahɇ   ruti*
    then happy-heart-very-they because was-they person-barren not

    žiʔnreni
    child-they

8. Then it was coming out, he said to Susläii, "There is a box coming to the shore of the ocean."

9. Then he said, "Let's see what is in the box."

10. When they took out the box, there were two children coming out of it.

11. Then he said, "Two children are coming out of there," he said.

12. Then they had very happy hearts because they did not have any children.

8. Cuando la vio exclamó: —¡Una caja viene en el mar!

9. Y su esposa le dijo: —Ve a sacarla para ver qué tiene adentro.

10. Cuando sacó la caja del mar, vio que adentro estaban dos niños.

11. Y dijo: —Aquí adentro hay dos niños.

12. Entonces los dos se alegraron mucho, porque ellos no podían tener niños.

13. *trabahW kadehDreni*
    suffering passing-they

14. *ǰehk rähpni   byuuxre saknäduš   nuure*
    then saying-he child-this will-be-with-very us

15. *dee gak   ži?nnu   rähpni*
    these will-be child-our saying-he

16. *ǰehk bastyoobni   rebyuužre*
    then caused-grow-he children-this

17. *rebyuužre raknähreni   risa?nreni ši   rahW*
    child-this being-with-they leaving-they what eating

    Golgisahre   naga?ni
    Golgisah-this is-lying-he

18. *guyu? stee   beh<u>N</u> ni   et   laadi   baliǰnireni*
    is   another person that not good-not advised-he-them

13. They were suffering much.

14. Then he said, "These children will help us very much.

15. These will be our children," he said.

16. Then he caused these children to grow.

17. These children were helping, they were taking to Golguisaj, who was lying down, what he would eat.

18. There was another person who did not give good advice to them.

13. Sufrían mucho.

14. Él dijo: —Estos niños nos ayudarán mucho.

15. Estos niños serán nuestros hijos —dijo él.

16. Entonces, criaron a los niños.

17. Los niños les ayudaban, le llevaban la comida a Golguisaj siempre que estaba acostado.

18. Pero después vino alguien que les dio un mal consejo a los niños.

19. *nahkni te benla¢yah*
    was-he one person-liar

20. *rähpni la?tu byuux kadedduštu   trabahW loh*
    saying-he you child passing-very-you suffering for

    dade?ga
    father-little-that

21. *et štaddituni   rähpni*
    not of-dad-not-your-him saying-he

22. *žo nahNlu   et štaddinuni*
    how is-know-you not of-dad-not-our-him

23. *rähpreni loh dade?re   syädroobnu*
    saying-they to father-little-this coming-grow-us

24. *žo dini gak štadnu*
    how not-he will-be of-dad-our

25. *dini gak štadtu*
    not-he will-be of-dad-your

19. He was a liar.

20. He said, "You children, you are
    undergoing much suffering for
    that little father.

21. He is not your father," he said.

22. "How do you know he is not
    our father?"

23. they said. "For this little father
    raised us.

24. How can he not be our father?"

25. "He is not your father.

19. Esta persona era mentirosa.

20. Les dijo: —Ustedes están sufrien-
    do mucho con ese señor.

21. Él no es el padre de ustedes
    —les dijo.

22. ¿Cómo sabes que él no es nues-
    tro padre?

23. —le dijeron— con él hemos cre-
    cido,

24. ¿cómo que no es nuestro padre?

25. —No es el padre de ustedes.

26. *narä nančeä   et   štaddituni*
    I   know-well-I not of-dad-not-you-he

27. *Luš te   kwääz trabahW ni   kadehDtu   mbahY nah*
    and one leave suffering that passing-you OK   now

    tedtu   te   giniä   žo   guntuni   te   kwääz
    will-pass-you that will-say-I how will-be-you-it one leave

    retrabahW
    sufferings

28. *žoni   xyennuni   rähpni*
    how-that will-do-we-it saying-he

29. *pal nahlu   et   štaddinuni   šlia?si   kadeednu*
    if say-you not of-dad-not-our-he vain-just passing-we

    trabahW rähp
    suffering saying

30. *xyäädtu   gižee   rähpni*
    will-come-you tomorrow saying-he

26. I know he is not your father.

27. And in order that you be free from suffering, OK now, you pass by in order that I will tell you how to do to him in order that you will be freed of sufferings."

28. "What shall we do?" he (child) said.

29. "If you say he is not our father, then this suffering is worthless."

30. "Stop by tomorrow," he (liar) said.

26. Yo sé muy bien que no es su padre.

27. Y para que ya no sigan sufriendo, vengan, les voy a decir qué pueden hacer para que ya no sufran.

28. —¿Qué haremos?—dijeron—.

29. Si dices que no es nuestro padre, entonces estamos sufriendo en balde.

30. —Pues vengan mañana —les dijo.

31. *če   bara yääl gudehDreni roʔk kadro sugaʔza*
    when early night passed-they there where will-lying-also

    behNre
    person-this

32. *badeed behNre   gaii dzutbehD   lohni*
    passed person-this five bone-turkey to-him

33. *jehk rähpni   ganid ʒutbehDre   gukwaatuni   yehk*
    then saying-he first bone-turkey-this will-nail-you-him head

    Golgisahre   rähpni
    Golgisah-this saying-he

34. *sas giraani gukwaatu   yehkni*
    and all-it   will-nail-you head-his

35. *kombast   ʒutbehDga   juʔt   behNre*
    that's-enough bone-turkey-that will-kill person-this

36. *čeni   get   behNre   če   aguht   behNre*
    when-it will-die person-this when already-died person-this

    jehkni   kwägahktu   lastooni rähpni
    then-that will-take-immediately-you heart-his saying-he

31. When daylight came, they went to where this person was.

32. This person gave some eggs to them.

33. Then he said, "Throw the first egg at Golguisaj's head," he said.

34. "And the rest of them, you throw at his head.

35. That is enough to kill him.

36. When you have killed him, take out his heart," he said.

31. Al día siguiente fueron a donde estaba esa persona.

32. Él les dio cinco huevos.

33. —Tiren el primer huevo a la cabeza de Golguisaj —les dijo—.

34. Y tiren los demás sobre él.

35. Eso basta para martarlo.

36. Cuando ya esté muerto, sáquenle el corazón —dijo.

37. *če   aguläätu   lastooni gučahtu   bäzbagih¢*
    when already-will-take-you heart-it will-fill-you bee-wasp

    beh<u>N</u>re   gäbtu   loh šnantu   štadä   bagu?t
    person-this will-say-you to of-mother-your of-dad-my killed

    te biʒuhN ni?k   gunlu   šweh gidaunu
    one deer   therefore will-be-you dinner will-eat-we

38. *mbah rähpreni   čonänuni*
    OK   saying-they go-with-we-it

39. *če   biʒuh<u>n</u>reni jehk rähpni   mamá rähpreni*
    when arrived-they then saying-he mother saying-they

    nilagaanlu   štadnu   bagu?t te   biʒuhN
    neither-will-know-you of-dad-our killed one deer

40. *<u>n</u>ah aree   lastoo biʒuhNr gunluni   šweh   rähpni*
    now already-here heart deer-this will-be-you-it dinner saying-he

41. *mbah*
    OK

37. "When you have taken out his heart, fill him with red wasps, tell your mother that your father killed a deer. Have her prepare dinner for you to eat."

38. "OK," they said, "we will go do it."

39. They went to their mother and told her that their father had killed a deer.

40. Now here was the heart of the deer for her to make a dinner out of it.

41. "OK."

37. Después que le saquen el corazón, llénenle el estómago de avispas rojas. Luego lleven el corazón a su mamá y díganle: "Nuestro padre mató un venado y quiere que hagas una comida con esto".

38. —Muy bien —dijeron los niños— lo haremos.

39. Cuando llegaron a la casa, el niño dijo: —¡Mamá!, fíjate que nuestro padre mató un venado.

40. Te traemos el corazón de ese venado para que hagas una comida.

41. —Bueno.

42. *šet   nahkdi   rähpni*
    not was-not saying-she

43. *nageste   gunäni*
    soon-that will-be-I-it

44. *sägahk   behNre   roʔ   geuu satiibni   žobdäh*
    go-immediately person-this mouth river washing-she corn-meal

45. *če   bižuhNni   roʔ   geuu rähp bež lohni   kauu kauu*
    when arrived-she mouth river saying frog to-her kauu kauu

    rähpni
    saying-it

46. *ǰehkni   rähpni   šikwent rnii   manre   skree*
    then-that saying-it why   saying animal-this way

47. *če   gunisak   bežre   kauu kauu ǰehk rähp   bežre*
    when said-again frog-this kauu kauu then saying frog-this

    pet   lagahk luh gauulu   lastoo čäällu
    maybe herself you will-eat-you heart spouse-your

42. "It is all right," she said.	42. Está bien —dijo ella—.
43. "I will make it soon."	43. Al ratito la hago.
44. She went to the river immediately to wash the corn meal.	44. Entonces la señora se fue al río a lavar su nixtamal.
45. When she arrived at the river a frog said to her, "Croak, croak." it said.	45. Y cuando llegó al río, una rana le dijo: —Croak, croak.
46. Then she said, "Why is this animal speaking this way?"	46. Y ella se preguntó: "¿Por qué dice eso este animal?"
47. Then this frog spoke again, "Croak, croak, maybe you yourself are going to eat your husband's heart."	47. Entonces le dijo la rana otra vez: —Croak, croak. Puede ser que vas a comer el corazón de tu esposo.

48. *roʔkni   gukbee   Susläiire   rähpni   yuʔča   ši*
    there-that made-straight Susläii-this saying-she is-perhaps what

    abiyehN   rebyuužre   štadreni
    already-did children-this of-dad-their

49. *če   biʒuhNni   jehk rähpni   kontu*
    when arrived-she then saying-she where-you

50. *rähpni   čowiinu   kon   štadtu   rähpni*
    saying-she go-see-we where of-dad-your saying-she

51. *če   syäädtu   kon   štadtu   rähpni*
    when coming-you where of-dad-your saying-she

52. *aštadnu   nagaʔ rähpreni*
    there-of-dad-our is-lying saying-they

53. *nah čowiinu   kon   štadtu   rähpni*
    now go-see-we where of-dad-your saying-she

48. Then Susläii imagined that was done and she said, "The children must have done something to their father."

48. Susläii entonces se imaginó que algo había pasado, y pensó: "Tal vez estos niños le hicieron algo a su papá".

49. When she arrived back to the house, she said, "Where are you?"

49. Cuando llegó a su casa les dijo: —¿Dónde están ustedes?

50. She said, "We are going to see where your father is," she said.

50. Y agregó: —Vamos a ver a su papá.

51. When they arrived, "Where is your father?" she asked.

51. ¿Dónde estaba su papá cuando vinieron? —les preguntó.

52. "Our father is lying over there," they said.

52. —Pues estaba allá acostado —dijeron.

53. "Now we are going to see where your father is," she said.

53. —Bueno, ahora vamos a ver dónde está su papá —dijo la mamá.

54. *če bizuhNni nagarloh   behNre*
    when arrived-she is-lying-face^to person-this

55. *šikwent nagarloh   štadtu   rähpni*
    why   is-lying-face^to of-dad-you saying-she

56. *čuh   dinu   gidon   rähpreni*
    who^knows not-we will-let's-see saying-they

57. *če byopsaʔnnu ši gauni   nagasahni   rähpreni*
    when are-left-we what will-eat-he is-lying-back-he saying-they

58. *dinu   gidon   rähpreni*
    not-we will-let's-see saying-they

59. *per šoditu   gan   rähpni*
    but how-not-you know saying-she

60. *ni laʔtu gižee   gižee   ryädsaʔntu   ši   gauni*
    that you tomorrow tomorrow coming-leave-you what ate-he

    rähpni
    saying-she

54. When they arrived, their father was lying face down.

55. "Why is your father lying face down?" she said.

56. "Why, we do not know," they said.

57. "When we came to leave him his dinner, he was lying face up," they said.

58. "We do not know," they said.

59. "But how did you not know?" she said.

60. "You come day after day bring his food," she said.

54. Cuando llegaron, el señor estaba acostado boca abajo.

55. —¿Por qué está su papá boca abajo? —les preguntó.

56. —¡Quién sabe! Nosotros no sabemos.

57. Cuando vinimos a traerle la comida estaba acostado boca arriba —respondieron—.

58. Nosotros no sabemos —dijeron.

59. —Pero, ¿cómo no van a saber?,

60. si ustedes le han traído de comer diario —les dijo—.

61. *mbah fiä   don   šiniʔk   rahk   štadtu*
    OK   will-see-I let's see what-therefore making of-dad-your

    rähpni
    saying-she

62. *jehk batyečloh   Susläiire   Golgisahre*
    then turned-over Susläii-this Golgisah-this

63. *če   biriyä̱l   rebäzbagihȼre Susläii gudauyaʔreni Susläii*
    when went-stung bee-wasps-this Susläii ate-bit-they   Susläii

    li   kabišät
    much knock^down

64. *jehk guhk bažu̱n   rebyuužre*
    then was running children-this

65. *čeni   bažu̱n rebyuužre   jehk rähpni   rebyuužre*
    when-that ran   children-this then saying-she children-this

    anahNreni   žo   guht čälä
    already-know-they how died spouse-my

61. "OK, I will see what happened
    to your father," she said.

61. Bueno, voy a ver qué es lo que
    tiene su papá —les dijo.

62. Then Susläii turned Golguisaj
    over.

62. Entonces Susläii volteó a Golgui-
    saj.

63. When there came out those
    wasps, they stung her and knock-
    ed Susläii down.

63. Y cuando lo volteó, salieron las
    avispas rojas y picaron tanto a
    Susläii que la hicieron revolcarse
    en el suelo.

64. Then it happened these children
    ran.

64. Esto aprovecharon los niños pa-
    ra correr.

65. Then those children ran away
    and she said, "Those children
    know how my husband died."

65. Pero cuando los niños corrieron,
    ella se dijo: "Estos niños saben
    cómo murió mi esposo.

66. *yuʔ šikwent bažuṉ rebyuužre   sääreni*
    is   why   ran   children-this going-they

67. *čadedä   part   šmbalä   aguht   rähpni*
    will-pass-I news of-<compadre>-my already-died saying-he

68. *če   bizuhNni   kon   mbaal   rähpni*
    when arrived-she where <compadre> saying-she

69. *narä syädnijä   part lo guehBlu   nani gusahk*
    I   coming-give-I news on mister-you that happen

    šmbaallu   rähpni
    of-<compadre>-your saying-she

70. *ši   gusahk šmbalä   <maal> rähpni*
    what happen of-<compadre>-my comadre saying-he

71. *nila   gaanlu   rähpni   ree syädnää   te   dijduš*
    neither know-you saying-she here coming-with-I one word-very

    jyendyahGlu   rähpni
    will-do-ear-you saying-she

66. Those children knew why they ran, they went.

66. Por eso se fueron corriendo.

67. "I am going to tell my <compadre> that my husband is dead," she said.

67. Voy a avisar a mi compadre que mi esposo ha muerto", dijo.

68. When she arrived, "Where are you my <compadre>?" she said.

68. Cuando llegó a donde su compadre, le dijo: —¿Dónde está usted compadre?

69. "I am coming to tell you about what happened to my husband," she said.

69. Aquí le vengo a contar lo que le pasó a su compadre —le dijo.

70. "What happened to my <compadre>, <comadre>?" he said.

70. —¿Qué le pasó a mi compadre, comadre? —le preguntó.

71. "Don't you know?" she said. "Here I am coming to bring you very bad news," she said.

71. —Ni sabe usted —le dijo—. Le traigo una noticia muy grave.

72. *šičaniʔk*
    what-perhaps-therefore

73. *šmbaallu*   *guht rähpni*
    of-<compadre>-your died saying-she

74. *beṇdaan*   *beṇdip*   *šmbalä*   *žo*
    person-strong person-healthy of-<compadre>-my how

    getni   *rähpni*
    will-die-he saying-he

75. *gujtni*   *rähpni*
    died-he saying-she

76. *čowiinu*
    go-see-we

77. *konza*   *rebyuux roʔk*
    where-also children there

72. "What is it?"

73. "Your <compadre> is dead,"
    she said.

74. "How can a strong healthy
    <compadre> die?" he said.

75. "He died," she said.

76. "Let's go see.

77. Where are the children?

72. —¿Qué será?

73. —Su compadre se murió —dijo
    ella.

74. —¿Cómo se va a morir mi com-
    padre, si él es una persona
    fuerte y sana? —le dijo.

75. —Pero se murió —dijo ella.

76. —Vamos a ver.

77. ¿Dónde están los niños?

78. *et gižee gižee yuʔ rebyuux sasaʔn ši gauni*
    not tomorrow tomorrow is children leaving what will-eat-he

    rähpni
    saying-he

79. *ṇah če byädnä rebyuužre te lastoo bizuhN rähp*
    now when came-with children-this one heart deer saying

    Susläii jehk waʔä roʔ geuu nah bez Kauu kauu
    Susläii then went-I mouth river say frog Kauu kauu

80. *jehkni gukbegakä lagahk naräča gauä*
    then-that made-know-immediately-I herself I-perhaps will-eat-I

    lastoo čälä rähpni
    heart spouse-I saying-she

81. *jehkni räpä loh rebyuužre čowiinu kon štadtu*
    then-that saying-I to children-this will-see-we where of-dad-you

78. Didn't the children take out
    what he would eat every day?"
    he said.

79. "Now when the children came
    with the heart of a deer," said
    Susläii, "I went to the river and
    a frog said 'Croak, croak'.

80. Then I knew immediately that
    perhaps I would eat the heart of
    my husband," she said.

81. "Then I said to the children,
    'Let's go see where your father
    is'.

78. ¿Qué, no diario le llevaban de
    comer? —le preguntó.

79. —Sí, pero hoy, cuando los niños
    me trajeron el corazón de un ve-
    nado para hacer la comida, me
    fui al río y allí me dijo una rana:
    "croak, croak".

80. Y luego me di cuenta de que a
    lo mejor me iba a comer el cora-
    zón de mi esposo —dijo ella—.

81. Entonces le dije a los niños: "Va-
    mos a ir a ver dónde está su
    papá".

82. *če   biẕunä   roʔk   aguht   behNre*
    when arrived-I there already-died person-this

83. *jehk gudauyaʔ bäzbagihɛre   narä jehkni   räpä   nah*
    then ate-bit   bee-wasp-this me   then-that saying-I now

    nahNtu   žo   guht   štadtu   räpä
    know-you how died of-dad-your saying-I

84. *roʔkti   bažun rebyuužre*
    there-just ran   children-this

85. *mbahY nah pal nahlu   siʔk abažun   rebyuužre roʔk*
    OK   now if   say-you like already-ran child-this there

    rkiin   regirdoob   štenlu maal   kooblu
    be-necessary stonesˆsuck   of-you comadre will-suck-you

    rebyuužre   rähpni
    children-this saying-he

86. *te   don   ši   kastiigw   gideednu   rebyuužre   rähpni*
    that let'sˆsee what punishment will-pass-we children-this saying-he

82. When I arrived there, this person was already dead.

83. Then those wasps stung me, then I said, 'Now you know how your father died'.

84. Just then those children ran."

85. "Well now if you say your children have run away like this, why don't you use your stone suck and suck the children back here," he said,

86. "in order we know what punishment we will give these children," he said.

82. Pero cuando llegué allí, él ya estaba muerto.

83. Y me picaron las avispas. Entonces les dije a los niños: "Ustedes saben cómo murió su padre".

84. Pero los niños se fueron corriendo.

85. —Si dice usted que corrieron los niños, pues entonces vamos a necesitar su piedra de chupar, comadre, para que chupe usted a los niños de vuelta— dijo él—.

86. Traiga a los niños para ver qué castigo les damos— le dijo.

87. *če   gudohBni gubi?   byuužre sa?ksi girdoobre*
    when sucked-she returned child-this because stone-suck-this

    lagahk ǰehk gubi?   rebyuux
    herself then returned children

88. *gunaluš   maal   rähpni*
    didn't^I^tell-you <comadre> saying-he

89. *n̠ah jyennu   kastiigw   rebyuužre*
    now will-do-we punishment children-this

90. *šikwent jyahBreni   sa? šigabre   ju?treni*
    why   will-fall-they kind thought-this will-kill-they

    šmbalä   rähpni   mbahY mbaal
    of-<compadre>-my saying-she OK   <compadre>

91. *xhetnahkdi jyennu   kastiigwreni*
    not-was-not will-do-we punishment-they

87. When she sucked on it, she sucked those children back immediately.

88. "Didn't I tell you <comadre>," he said.

89. "Now we will punish these children."

90. "Why did these children have this thought to kill my husband?" she asked. "OK <compadre>.

91. It does not matter, we will punish these children.

87. Y cuando ella chupó la piedra, los niños regresaron, porque esa piedra de chupar los trajo inmediatamente.

88. —¿Ya ve usted? —dijo él—.

89. Ahora vamos a castigar a estos niños.

90. Porque estos niños mataron a mi compadre. —Bueno, compandre,

91. no importa. Vamos a castigar a estos niños.

92. *nah narä gäpä   lohreni čaca?reni   gaii yehG te*
    now I   will-say-I to-them will-bring-they five wood that

    gize?knu   ya
    will-burn-we sweat^house

93. *nen yaga   gigu?tnuni   rähpni   ni?k*
    in   sweat^house-that will-kill-we-him saying-she therefore

    nanab gakreni   rähpni
    deserve will-be-they saying-she

94. *mbahY šet nahkdi*
    OK   not was-not

95. *jehk rähpni   čaca?tu   gaii yahG ži?nä   te*
    then saying-she will-bring-you five wood child-my that

    yare   sa?csi kayumaläre
    sweat^house-this because am-sick-I-this

92. Now I will tell them to bring some wood and we will heat the sweat house.

93. In the sweat house we will kill them," she said, "because this is what they deserve," she said.

94. "It does not matter."

95. Then she said (to the children), "Get some wood so that I can enter the sweat house because I am sick."

92. Ahorita les voy a decir que traigan leña para el temascal.

93. Y dentro del temascal los matamos, porque eso es lo que se merecen— dijo ella.

94. —Está muy bien.

95. Entonces ella les dijo a los niños: —Vayan a traer leña para que yo me meta en el temascal, porque estoy enferma.

96. *šet nahkdi mbahY mamá čacaʔäni   pal nahlu siʔk*
    not was-not OK   mother will-bring-I-it if   say-you like

    čacaʔäni   rähp   byuužga
    will-bring-I-it saying child-that

97. *če   biẕunnähni   yahGga   agukbee   byuužre*
    when arrived-with-it wood-that already-made-straight child-this

    šiniʔk   gun   šnanni   niʔk   ganiddoo byuʔ
    what-therefore will-be of-mother-his therefore first-big   was

    byuux nigiiga   nen ya   guẕuhDni te   geed kwä'
    child man-that in   sweat^house drilled-he one hole side

    ya
    sweat^house

98. *jehk rähpni   pet   juʔtča   šnannu   nuure*
    then saying-he maybe will-kill-perhaps of-mother-our us

    čunu nen ya   räjpni   mbah nah rähpni
    be-we in   sweat^house saying-he OK   now saying-he

    čonänu   gaii batoob
    go-with-we five maguey^leaf

96. "Well, Mother, I will go get the wood if you say so," he (child) said.

97. When he arrived with the wood he already told his sister what his mother would do. The boy went into the sweat house and drilled a hole in the bottom.

98. Then he said, "Our mother will kill us in the sweat house. Let's go get some maguey leaves.

96. —Cómo no, mamá, ahorita se la traemos— le dijo el niño.

97. Cuando llegaron con la leña, como ya sabían lo que les iba a hacer su mamá, el muchachito entró primero al temascal e hizo un hoyo en la base del temascal.

98. Entonces dijo: —Nuestra madre nos va a matar echándonos dentro del temascal. Por eso, vamos a buscar algunas pencas de maguey.

99. *če   gizuNnu   ganiddoo batoob   gizälnu   nen*
    when will-arrive-we first-big   maguey^leaf will-throw-we in

    ya   rähpni
    sweat^house saying-he

100. *če   naani jyuʔnu   ǰehk jyuʔnu   nenga*
    when say-she will-are-we then will-are-we in-that

101. *narä giriä   stelaad   kadro guzudä   geed roʔk*
    I   will-go-I other^side where will-drill-I hole there

    giriyalä   rähpni
    will-go-quickly-I saying-he

102. *ǰehk ·jyädnalgahklu   narä rähpni*
    then will-come-follow-immediately-you me   saying-he

99. When we return, I will throw them into the sweat house," he said.

100. "When she tells us to enter it, we will go in.

101. I will come out the other side where I drilled the hole, there I will come out quickly," he said.

102. "Then you follow quickly after me," he said.

99. Y cuando lleguemos, primero eché las pencas dentro del temascal— dijo él—.

100. Y cuando nos diga que entremos, entraré.

101. Entonces, saldré por el otro lado, por el hoyo que hice —dijo—.

102. Y luego, tú me sigues.

103. *če   byuʔ byuux nigiire   nen̲ ya   birigahkni*
     when was   child man-this in sweatˆhouse went-immediately-he

     stelaad   nez kwä' ya   sanal̲gahk
     otherˆside way side sweatˆhouse following-immediately

     ĵapeʔreni
     girl-little-this-him

104. *ĵehk gusloh rebatoobre   kayeča?*
     then began magueyˆleaves-this banging

105. *giraa rešigab ni byahBtu šigab baguʔttu štadtu*
     all   thoughts that fall-you thought killed-you of-dad-your

     mbahY n̲ah rähpni   roʔk sigahkza col̲kihžni n̲ah
     OK   now saying-she there like-also youˆpay-it now

     siʔktis   šigab ni byahBtu
     like-manner thought that fall-you

106. *awii   žo kayeča? yehkre rebyuužre mbaal*
     already-see how banging head-this children-this <compadre>

     rähpni
     saying-she

103. When the boy went into the sweat house, he went through to the other side and immediately this little girl followed him.

104. Then the maguey leaves started banging.

105. Their mother said, "All the thoughts you had to kill your father are being repaid you.

106. Look how the heads of the children are thundering, <compadre>," she said.

103. Cuando el muchachito entró al temascal y salió por el otro lado, la muchachita lo siguió inmediatamente.

104. Entonces, las pencas de maguey comenzaron a tronar.

105. —Ahora sí —dijo la mamá— van a pagar todo el mal que le hicieron a su padre.

106. Oiga cómo truenan las cabezas de los niños, compadre —dijo.

107. *jehk birii   šmbaalni   rähp   ni?k nahk nani*
     then came^out of-<compadre>-her saying this was   that

     nungähL rebyuužre   kayeča? yobyehkreni
     deserve   children-this banging brain-head-their

108. *jehk birigahk   Susläii sawii   kon   reštrastni*
     then went-immediately Susläii go-seeing where of-things-her

     reš¢uhBni   reni   runnähni   ʒuun
     of-needles-her they being-with-she work

109. *če   biʒuhNni   šeti š¢uhBni   kadro yučee*
     when arrived-she not of-needle-her where is-made

     š¢uhBni   šeti škiwahNni   šeti bähkw štenni šeti
     of-needle-her not of-mirror-her not comb of-her not

110. *jehkni   rähpni   nikla ganlu   mbaal   šeti*
     then-that saying-she neither will-know-you <compadre> not

     reštrastä   rähpni
     of-things-I saying-she

107. Then her <compadre> said, "These were deserving children, their brains are banging."

108. Then Susläii went to get her belongings, her weaving needles that she used in her work.

109. When she arrived, she could not find her weaving needle, her mirror nor her comb.

110. Then she said to her <compadre>, "I cannot find my things."

107. Y el compradre le contestó —Eso es lo que merecen estos niños: que les truenen los sesos.

108. Luego Susläii fue a buscar sus pertenencias, sus agujas que usaba para tejer.

109. Pero cuando llegó, no pudo encontrar ni sus agujas ni su espejo ni su peine.

110. Entonces ella le dijo a su compadre: —Fíjese que no encuentro mis cosas.

111. *giwiinu   nen ya   donnu   kon   rebyuux rähpni*
will-see-we in   sweat^house let's-see-we where children saying-he

112. *če   bawiireni con   rebyuux*
when saw-they   where children

113. *laa   rebatoob   ni   kayeča?*
good   maguey^leaves that banging

114. *kayeča? yehk rebatoobga*
banging head maguey^leaves-that

115. *ču   rebyuužre*
who children-this

116. *rähpni   pet   benjab   rebyuužre*
saying-he maybe person-evil children-this

117. *awii   nah abirii   rebyuužre*
already-see now already-came^out children-this

111. "Let's go to the sweat house to see if the children are there," he said.

112. When they looked, where were the children?

113. They saw only maguey leaves banging.

114. The leaves of the maguey were just banging.

115. "Whose children are these?"

116. He said, "Maybe these children are devils."

117. They saw now that the children had already come out.

111. —Pues vamos a buscar dentro del temascal, a ver cómo están los niños —dijo él.

112. Pero cuando miraron dentro del temascal no vieron a los niños.

113. Sólo vieron las pencas de maguey tronando.

114. Pues sólo eran las pencas de maguey que tronaban.

115. —¿Quiénes son estos niños?

116. Tal vez son demonios —dijo él.

117. Entonces vieron que los niños se haban salido.

118. *et   laati   rebyuužre   ni   kayeča? yehkni   rähpni*
     not good-just children-this that banging head-his saying-he

     rebatoobre   ni   kayeča?
     maguey^leaves-this that banging

119. *rebyuuže?   kwa?   girdoobre   bačahreni giin nen̲*
     children-little will-take stone-suck-this filled-they chile in

     girdoobre
     stone-suck-this

120. *regimbihZ bačahreni nen̲ni*
     chiles-dry filled-they in-it

121. *mbaal   rähpni   rahplu   girdoob   rähpni*
     <compadre> saying-he having-you stone-suck saying-he

118. "It is not the heads of the children banging," he said, "it was just the maguey leaves."

119. Those little children had filled the stone suck with hot dry chile.

120. Dry chiles they put in it.

121. Then the godfather said, "You have the stone suck.

118. —No eran sus cabezas las que tronaban —dijo él—. Sólo eran estas pencas de maguey.

119. Mientras tanto, los niños ya habían preparado la piedra de chupar: la habían llenado de chiles secos.

120. Con chiles secos y picantes la habían llenado.

121. —Pues, comadre —dijo el compadre—, usted tiene todavía su piedra de chupar.

122. *ŋah   gidoobnu   rebyuužre   stee   te   roʔk   donnu*
     now   will-suck-we   children-this   again   that   there   let's-see-we

     ši   kastiigw   gideednuni   stee   rähpni
     what   punishment   will-pass-we-them   another   saying-he

123. *gudohB Susläii neŋ girdoobre   stee   če   wäʼp giinga*
     sucked   Susläii   in   stone-suck-this   again   when   went   chile-that

     yehkni   ameer   nyehtni
     head-her   almost   almost^die-she

124. *ŋah abehN   rebyuužre   gaan narä saʔksi   pet*
     now   already-made   children-this   knew   I   because   maybe

     benǰab   nahk rebyuužre
     person-evil   was   children-this

125. *awii   abašiinreni   girdoob   štenä*
     already-see   already-spoiled-they   stone-suck   of-I

122. Now we will suck these children again in order we will know what punishment to give them," he said.

123. Susläii sucked the stone but the chile went into her head so that she almost died.

124. Now she said, "These children have already beat me, they must be the devil.

125. They have already spoiled my stone suck.

122. Vamos a jalar otra vez a estos niños para ver qué castigo les vamos a dar —dijo él.

123. Así que, Susläii usó otra vez su piedra de chupar, pero al chuparla, el chile se le subió hasta la cabeza y por poco se muere.

124. —Ahora sí —dijo ella— estos niños me han ganado; puede ser que sean demonios.

125. Echaron a perder hasta mi piedra de chupar.

126. *šetru   gakti   gunä   rähpni   saʔksi   diru*
     not-more   will-be-just   will-be-I   saying-she   because   not-more

     girdoob   gun   sirb   par   narä   rähpni
     stone-suck   will-be   serve   for   me   saying-she

127. *narä gusaksiä   rebyuužre   maal   rähpni*
     I   will-punish-I   children-this   comadre   saying-he

128. *kon   narä gak   reglaadni*
     where   I   will-be   arrange-it

129. *Luš šmbaalni   te   bälduš   nahk*
     and of-<compadre>-her   one   snake-very   was

     šmbaalni
     of-<compadre>-her

130. *če   birii   šmbaalni   jehk rähpni*
     when   came^out   of-<compadre>-her   then   saying-he

     čanalä   rebyuužre
     will-follow-I   children-this

126. There is nothing I can do," she said, "because my stone suck does not work for me.

127. "I will punish these children, <comadre>," he said.

128. "I will arrange for it."

129. And her <compadre> was a big snake.

130. Then her <compadre> said, "I will go follow the children."

126. Y como mi piedra de chupar no sirve, ya no puedo hacer nada — dijo ella.

127. —Pues yo castigaré a esos niños, comadre —dijo el compadre—.

128. Conmigo se arreglará el asunto.

129. El compadre se convirtió en una culebra muy grande.

130. Cuando salió, dijo: —Voy a seguir a esos niños.

131. *saʔksi   rebyuužre   asanäreni   rezuhB näh*
     because children-these already-going-with-they needles with

     reyagžigäälre   näh bähkw näh giwahNre
     woods-know-night-this with comb with stone-mirror-this

     niʔkni   če   bawiirenini rähpreni šmbaal
     therefore-that when saw-they-him saying-they of-<compadre>

     šnannu   syädnahL   nuure rähpreni
     of-mother-our coming-follow us   saying-they

132. *žo   jyennu   rähpreni*
     how will-do-we saying-they

133. *če   bakwaalreni zuhB te   lagunduš guhk zuhBre*
     when threw-they   needle one lake-very was needle-this

134. *roʔk guklaa   bälre   lalni   gunihDrureni   lohni*
     there made-long snake-this while-that will-pass-more-they to-him

135. *jehktiru   behN bälre   gaan biriini   lo lagunre*
     then-just-more made snake-this knew came^out-he on lake-this

131. Because these children were taking the machete, the weaving needle, the comb, and the mirror with them, when they saw their mother's <compadre> following, they said,

132. "What will we do?"

133. When they threw the machete, it became a great lake.

134. They made the snake go around the lake while they continued to move forward.

135. Soon the snake came around the lake.

131. Porque los niños se habían llevado el machete, la aguja de tejer, el peine y el espejo, cuando vieron al compadre que les seguía, dijeron: —¡El compadre de nuesta madre nos viene siguiendo!

132. ¿Qué haremos?

133. Entonces tiraron el machete y se convirtió en una laguna muy grande.

134. Y allí se entretuvo la culebra, porque tuvo que dar la vuelta al lago, mientras ellos avanzaban un poco más.

135. Entonces, la culebra rodeó la laguna.

136. *če   bawiireni abälre   syädnalsak*
     when saw-they already-snake-this coming-follow-again

137. *nah sii pet   sahW bälre   nuure*
     now yes maybe will-eat snake-this us

138. *mbah donnu   laa yuʔ ši   gibišloh*
     OK   let's-see-we QM is   what will-change-to

     yagžigäälre
     wood-knows-night-this

139. *če   bakwaani yagžigääl   guhk yagžigäälre*
     when nailed-he wood-knows-night was wood-knows-night-this

     te   bijukduš
     one vine-very

140. *roʔk guklaa   bälre   lalni   bažunreni sääreni*
     there made-long snake-this while-that ran-they   going-they

     zihtru
     far-more

136. When they looked, already the snake was following them again.

137. "Now the snake will eat us.

138. OK, now we will see what this needle will change to."

139. When they threw the needle, it became a great vine.

140. There the snake was delayed while they were running a little farther.

136. Cuando se dieron cuenta, la culebra ya los estaba siguiendo otra vez.

137. —Ahora sí que nos va a comer la culebra.

138. Bueno, vamos a ver si esta aguja de tejer se convierte en algo.

139. Cuando tiraron la aguja de tejer, se convirtió en una enredadera muy grande.

140. Allí la culebra perdió más tiempo. Mientras tanto, ellos corrieron más lejos.

141. *če   bawiireni asyädnal̲sak   bäl̲re   laareni*
     when saw-they already-coming-follow-again snake-this them

142. *saa   bakwaani bähGWre guhk bähGWre stee   bijuk*
     then nailed-he comb-this was comb-this another vine

     maazru   lasdiht maazru   tupid
     more-more thin   more-more dense

143. *mbah n̲ah rähpni   kayaknäh giraa retrast štee šnannu*
     OK   now saying-he going-with all   things of   of-mother-our

     nuure
     us

144. *mbah n̲ah giniidrunu*
     OK   now will-advance-more-we

145. *če   bawiireni giwahNtis   sanäreni   Luš gahš*
     when saw-they stone-mirror-manner going-with-they and near

     bäzlul̲   asyääd   bäl̲
     little-little already-coming snake

141. When they looked, the snake was again following them.

142. Now they threw the comb and it became a thinner vine and more dense.

143. "Well now," he said, "Our mother's things are helping us.

144. We are going a little further."

145. And when they knew that they had only the mirror left, then the snake was again coming close.

141. Pero cuando volvieron a mirar, la culebra los seguía de nuevo.

142. Entonces, tiraron el peine, que se convirtió en otra enredadera más delgada y más tupida.

143. —Bueno, pues —dijo—, todos las cosas de nuestra madre nos han servido.

144. Ahora, vámonos más lejos.

145. Luego se dieron cuenta de que lo único que les quedaba era el espejo, y la culebra ya venía muy cerquita.

146. *nah   sii   rähpni   šetru   k aʔdinu   rähpni*
     now yes saying-he not-more will-go-not-we saying-he

147. *nah   sii   sahW   bälre   nuure*
     now yes will-eat snake-this us

148. *mbah   rähpni   lultis   giwahNre   caʔä*
     OK   saying-he last-manner stone-mirror-this will-go-I

     donnu   šiniʔk   gaknäj   giwahNre
     let's-see-we what-therefore will-be-with stone-mirror-this

149. *pal gaknäj   giwahNre   nuure ǰehk sii*
     if   will-be-with stone-mirror-this us   then yes

     abyennu   gaan   rähpni
     already-made-we will-know saying-he

150. *per par šeti nah sii sahW   bälre   nuure*
     but for not now yes will-eat snake-this us

146. "Now the only thing left is to see if the mirror can help us," he (child) said.

147. "Now this snake will eat us.

148. OK, the only thing to do is to see if the mirror will help us.

149. If this mirror helps us, then we will have won," he said.

150. "If not, then this snake will eat us."

146. —Ahora sí, lo único que nos queda es el espejo. A ver si puede ayudarnos —dijo el niño—.

147. O la culebra nos va a comer.

148. —Lo último que nos queda es este espejo; a ver en qué nos ayuda.

149. Porque si nos ayuda este espejo, habremos ganado —dijo el niño.

150. Pero si no, ahora sí que nos come la culebra.

151. *če   bakwaani giwahNre   gubišloj   giwahNre*
     when nailed-he stone-mirror-this changed-to stone-mirror-this

     guhkni te   giboduš
     was-it one   stone-fire-very

152. *galäiiga   bijya?n   bä̲l*
     middle-that went-remained snake

153. *ro?ti gunitloh bä̲l*
     there passed-to snake

154. *mbah n̲ah sii rähpni   abyennu   gaan n̲ah*
     OK   now yes saying-he already-made-we knew now

     čosaanu   nez ree rähpni
     go-walk-we way here saying-he

155. *sasah   giropreni niluš ǰape?re   abaǰahGni*
     walking two-they then girl-little-this already-tired-she

     syädsahni
     coming-walk-she

151. When they threw the mirror, it became a great fire.

152. The snake was in the middle.

153. It killed the snake.

154. "Now we know we are safe, now let's walk from here," he said.

155. The two of them walked along, the girl got tired as she walked.

151. Cuando el muchacho tiró el espejo, se convirtió en un fuego muy grande.

152. Y la culebra se quedó allí, en medio del fuego.

153. Y el fuego la mató.

154. Entonces dijeron: —Ahora sí, estamos a salvo. Vamos a caminar hacia adelante.

155. Los dos iban caminando, pero la muchachita se cansó de tanto caminar.

156. *diruni   gun   want   yälryohLni   kayohLni*
     not-more-she will-be travel thirstingly-she thirsting-she

157. *če   bizuhNni roʔ   te   bisyebäz yuʔ te   boʔk nis*
     when   arrived-she mouth one well-little is one little water

     ni   guʔni
     that drank-she

158. *li   gubihz nisga*
     much dried   water-that

159. *dini   gun want yälryohL*
     not-she be stand thirstingly

160. *žoni   jyennu   te gidaru   nisre*
     how-that will-do-we that will-come-more water-this

161. *narä kayoldušä   nis   rähpni*
     I   thirsting-very-I water saying-she

156. As they went along the girl was very tired and thirsty.	156. Y le dio tanta sed, que ya no podía aguantar.
157. When they arrived at a little well, she drank a little water.	157. Llegaron a un pocito que tenía un poco de agua, y ella tomó un poco.
158. The well dried up quickly.	158. Pero el agua se acabó pronto.
159. She could not stand to be thirsty.	159. Y ella no aguantaba la sed otra vez.
160. "What will we do in order to get more water?"	160. —¿Qué haremos para conseguir más agua?
161. "I am very thirsty for water," she said.	161. Porque tengo mucha sed —dijo—.

162. *jehk rähp jape?re   narä gunä   te   sakrifis*
     then saying girl-little-this I   will-be-I one sacrifice

     donnu   top   sidaru   nisre   stebo?k
     let's-see-we maybe will-come-more water-this more-little

163. *pwes žo   nahk sacrifis ni   gunlu*
     well how was   sacrifice that will-be-you

164. *kwää   te   laad baloä   rähpni*
     will-take-I one side eye-my saying-she

165. *jehk rähpni   sahkza   kwääluni*
     then saying-he will-make-also will-take-you-it

166. *top   si?k gak   gidaru   stebo?k   nis*
     maybe like will-be will-come-more more-little water

167. *če   nibääni   balohni biʒuhN̲ te   bengool   ro?k*
     when almost-take-she eye-her arrived one person-old there

162. Then this little girl said, "I will
     make a sacrifice in order that
     maybe more water will come
     out."

163. "What kind of a sacrifice will
     you make?"

164. "I will take out one eye," she said.

165. Then he said, "Well then remove it.

166. Maybe a little more water will
     come out."

167. She was getting ready to take
     out one of her eyes when an old
     man arrived there.

162. Creo que haré un sacrificio, a
     ver si así puede haber más agua
     en el pozo.

163. —¿Qué clase de sacrificio vas a
     hacer?

164. —Me sacaré un ojo —dijo ella.

165. Entonces dijo él: —Pues, hazlo.

166. A ver si así sale otro poco de
     agua.

167. Pero cuando ya se iba a sacar el
     ojo, llegó un anciano.

168. *šini?k   gunlu   byuux rähni*
     what-therefore will-be-you child saying-he

169. *jehk rähpni   narä dina gunä want yälry ohL̲ rähpni*
     then saying-she I   not-I be-I stand thirstily   saying-she

170. *te   si?k sahk   gidaru   nis   gunä   sakrifis*
     that like will-make will-come-more water will-be-I sacrifice

     kwää   te   laad baloä te   gidaru   nisre
     will-take-I one side eye-my that will-come-more water-this

     stebo?k   rähpni
     more-little saying-she

171. *na?k gunlu   si?k*
     no   will-do like

172. *palga gunlu   si?k agunihtlu   rähpni   sa?ksi*
     if-that will-be-you like already-will-pass-you saying-he because

     luh nungähL gaklu   bäii gusanihlu   yääl
     you deserve will-be-you moon will-shine-you night

168. "What are you doing child?" he said.	168. —¿Qué vas a hacer, muchacha? —le dijo.
169. Then she said, "I cannot stand to be thirsty," she said.	169. Y ella respondió: —Ya no aguanto la sed —dijo.
170. "In order that more water will come out, I will sacrifice one of my eyes," she said.	170. Y continuó: —Ya no aguanto la sed, y voy a hacer un sacrificio para que haya más agua en el pozo.
171. "Don't you do it.	171. —No lo hagas.
172. If you do this, you will be lost," he said, "because you are necessary; you will be the moon that shines at night.	172. Si lo haces, estás perdida, porque tú has sido destinada a ser la Luna que alumbra en la noche.

173. *Luš byuuž nigiire   gak   gubihǰ ni   rgusanih   rǰee rähpni*
     and child man-this will-be sun   that will-shine day saying-he

174. *ǰehk   ähpni   kagusgeelu   nuure rähpni*
     then saying-he causing-lie-you us   saying-she

175. *šoš nahNlu   jyaʔknuni*
     how is-know-you will-be-we-it

176. *saʔksi siʔk nungähL narä kaniä   niʔk   gaktu*
     because like necessary I   saying-I therefore will-be-you

     rähpni
     saying-he

177. *mbah rähpni   palga guliilu   gaknuni   palga*
     OK   saying-she if-that will-straight-you will-be-we-it if-that

     guliilu   gakä   bäii bisyanä   gak   gubihǰ šet
     will-straight-you will-be-I moon brother-my will-be sun   not

     nahkdi pal siʔk nungähL šet nahkdi gaknuni   rähpni
     was-not if   like necessary not was-not will-be-we-it saying-she

173. And the boy will be the sun that shines during the day," he said.

174. Then she said, "You are lying to us," she said.

175. "How do you know what we will be?"

176. "Because it is necessary, I am speaking to you," he said.

177. "Well," she said, "if you speak the truth, we will be this. If you say I will be the moon and my brother will be the sun, if we are destined, well it does not matter," she said.

173. Y este niño será el Sol, el cual alumbrará de día —le dijo.

174. Entonces la niña le dijo: —Tú nos estás engañando.

175. ¿Cómo sabes que estamos destinados para eso?

176. —Yo se los estoy diciendo porque para eso están destinados —les dijo.

177. —Bueno —dijo ella—, sí es cierto que yo seré la Luna y que mi hermano será el Sol, ni modo. Ya estamos destinados para eso. Esta bien.

178. *čušluj   rähpni*
     who-you saying-she

179. *ĵehk birii   dad   bengoolre   rähpni   narä nakä*
     then came^out father person-old-this saying-he I   is-be-I

     Gebdios
     Mister-God

180. *kaninää   laʔtu rähpni*
     saying-with-I you   saying-he

181. *anungäjLtu*
     already-necesary-you

182. *šet nahkdi rähpni*
     not was-not saying-she

183. *pwes niʔkti   nahk kwent šte bäii   näh šte gubihĵ*
     well therefore-just was   story of moon with of sun

184. *niʔkti   nahk kwentbäz ni   nanä*
     therefore-just was   story-little that know-I

178. "Who are you?" she said.

179. Then this old man said, "I am
     the real god.

180. I am speaking to you," he said.

181. "You are destined."

182. "It does not matter," she said.

183. This is the story of the moon
     and of the sun.

184. This is all of the little story I
     know.

178. —¿Quién es usted? —ella le pre-
     guntó.

179. Y aquel anciano le contestó
     —Yo soy el verdadero Dios.

180. Y yo les digo que ustedes

181. ya están destinados.

182. —No importa —dijo ella.

183. Pues, éste es el cuento de la
     Luna y el Sol.

184. Este es todo el corto cuento que
     yo sé.

John the Charcoal Maker

Jerómino Quero

1. *guyuʔ te beh<u>N</u> ni laa   Juan*
   is   one person that name^is John

2. *te ǰeh sobgaʔ Juan roʔ   šyuʔni*
   one day sit-lying John mouth of-house-his

3. *dini ga<u>n</u>   ši   gunni*
   not-he will-know what will-be-he

1. There was a man named John.	1. Éste era un hombre que se llamaba Juan.
2. One day he was sitting at the door of his house.	2. Un día estaba Juan sentado a la puerta de su casa
3. He did not know what he would do.	3. sin saber que hacer.

41

4. *jehk byahBni šigab*
   then fell-he   thought

5. *jehk rähpni nah sii nanä šini?k   gunä*
   then saying-he now yes know-I what-therefore will-be-I

6. *ča?ä   čato?ä   boo   balke   rebur   naliib rek*
   will-go-I will-sell-I charcoal many-little donkeys is-tie there

   šeti š̶uunreni
   not of-work-they

7. *niluš Juan dini gičaglahZ   gunni   ʒuun di*
   then John not-he will-gather-want will-be-he work not

   rlahZni   čaka?ni   yahG
   wanting-he will-bring-he wood

8. *jehkti   guslohni batohpni bogehD   ni ralgih lo däh*
   then-just began-he piled-he charcoal-pine that burn to kitchen

4. He had a thought.

5. Then he said "Yes, I know what I will do.

6. I will go sell charcoal, for there are many donkeys tied there that have no work."

7. But John did not like to work, he did not like to gather wood.

8. Then he started to gather pitch pine that is burned in the kitchen.

4. De repente tuvo una idea,

5. y dijo: —¡Ya sé lo que voy a hacer!

6. Iré a vender carbón ya que hay muchos burros por aquí sin hacer nada.

7. Pero como Juan era muy flojo, tenía mucha flojera de ir a traer leña.

8. Entonces, empezó a juntar palitos y olotes. Cosas que se pudieran quemar en la cocina.

9. *baze?kni   šyu?   rebur   baze?kni   giragahG   reyahG*
   burned-he of-house donkeys burned-he all-immediately woods

   ni   yu?   rolihZni   näh   giraa   reyaan
   that is   house-his with   all   wood

10. *stuje?nsi   nuze?kni   näh   šyu?ni   te   si?k*
    for^little-just almost-burn-he with of-house-his that like

    behNni   gaan   basnaani   boo
    made-he knew caused-hand-he charcoal

11. *kom   čäälni   rahp   gaii behD   jehk   rähpni*
    because spouse-his having five turkey then saying-he

    čanää   teh   rebehDre   te   guto?äni   te   maske
    will-with-I one ṭurkeys-these that will-sell-I-it that even-little

    te   xihG kafee   ška?ä
    one cup   coffee will-bring-I

9. He burned the donkey's corral;
   he burned all the wood that was
   in his house; he burned all the
   pine.

10. For a little he would have
    burned his own house in order
    to get his hand on charcoal.

11. Because his wife had some
    turkeys, he said to her, "I will
    take one of these to sell just to
    buy one cup of coffee."

9. Quemó el corral de los burros,
   quemó toda la madera que había en su casa, y todos los
   palitos.

10. Casi quema también su casa pa-
    ra poder juntar el carbón que
    quería.

11. Como su esposa tenía unos gua-
    jolotes, Juan le dijo: —Tengo
    que llevarme también un guajolo-
    te para venderlo, y poder
    comprar una taza de café.

12. *čeni   baluužni   basguuni   boo   dehȼ rebur*
    when-that finished-he caused-load-he charcoal back donkeys

    jehk baȼuubni behD lo jyaa   booga
    then put-he   turkey on above charcoal-that

13. *jehkti   birii   Juan*
    then-just came^out John

14. *čeni   bizuhN Juan lo te   gehj gudehDni rolihZ te*
    when-that arrived John to one town passed-he house one

    behN ni ruwah xqijehkni rähpni   la dilu   sii
    person that cutting of-hair-his saying-he QM not-you buy

    boo
    charcoal

15. *jehk gunabdiij dadeʔga   lak sahk   te   kargwni*
    then asked-word father-little-that how will-make one cargo-it

16. *jehk baluiini   kargw ni syädnä   behD*
    then showed-he cargo that coming-with turkey

12. When he finished loading the charcoal on the back of the donkey, he put the turkey on top of the charcoal.

13. Then he left.

14. When John arrived in a town he passed by a person who cuts hair and he said to him, "Won't you buy some charcoal?"

15. Then the barber asked him, "How much would one load cost?"

16. He saw the cargo that was coming with the turkey.

12. Cuando terminó de cargar el carbón en los burros, puso el guajolote encima del carbón.

13. Y entonces salió.

14. Al otro día Juan llegó a un pueblo, y cuando pasó por una peluquería le dijo al peluquero: —¿No compras carbón?

15. El peluquero le preguntó cuánto valía la carga,

16. señalando la carga debajo del guajolote.

17. *ĵehk rähp Juan sahkni čon gayuu beež*
    then saying John will-make-it three hundred peso

18. *ĵehk rähp dadeʔga basyähtni don*
    then saying father-little-that caused-disembark-it let'sasee

19. *ĵehk basyäht Juanni basuhtini behD stelaad*
    then caused-disembark John-it sat-just-he turkey more-place

    badeedtini boo lo dadeʔga
    passed-just-he charcoal to father-little-that

20. *ĵehk rähp dadeʔga lohni behDga karo basuhluni*
    then saying father-little-that to-him turkey-that where sat-you-it

21. *sapä te jinääni rähpni*
    tending-I that go-with-I-it saying-he

22. *ĵehk rähp dadeʔga žo nahkni pwes*
    then saying father-little-that how was-it well

17. Then John said, "It sells for three hundred pesos."

18. Then the barber was content and told him to unload it.

19. Then John unloaded it and set the turkey to one side.

20. Then the barber said to John, "Where did you put the turkey?"

21. "I have it over here so that I can take it with me," he said.

22. Then the barber said, "How is this, OK?"

17. Juan le dijo que valía trescientos pesos.

18. El peluquero se puso contento y le dijo: —Bájala pues.

19. Juan bajó el guajolote, lo puso a un lado, y entregó el carbón al peluquero.

20. Pero el peluquero protestó, diciendo: —¿Y el guajolote?

21. —Pues, lo hice a un lado porque tengo que llevármelo —dijo Juan.

22. —¿Cómo está eso? —dijo el peluquero.

23. *la   šetnähdi   behDga   gutonählu   boo*
    QM not-with-not turkey-that bought-with-you charcoal

24. *ni   lagahk   luh   nahlu   čon   gayuu   beež   sahk*
    that yourself you say-you three hundred peso will-make

    behDga   kon   boo
    turkey-that with charcoal

25. *ǰehk   rähp   Juan   per   dina   niniä   gutoʔä   behDga   kon*
    then saying John but not-I almost-say-I sold-I turkey-that with

    booga   siʔk
    charcoal-that like

26. *ši   nahlu   lak   sahk   te   behD   ree*
    what say-you how will-make one turkey here

27. *la   sahkni   čon   gayuu   kon   boo*
    QM will-make-it three hundred with charcoal

28. *dini   čää   siʔk*
    not-it will-go like

23. "It was not with the turkey that you bought the charcoal."

24. "Didn't you say 300 pesos for the turkey and the charcoal?"

25. Then John said, "But I did not say that I would sell that turkey with the charcoal like that."

26. "But what do you think one turkey would sell for?"

27. "Would it sell for three hundred pesos with the charcoal?"

28. "It does not go for that."

23. —No compraste el guajolote con el carbón —le dijo Juan.

24. —¿No dijiste que el carbón valía trescientos junto con el guajolote?

25. Juan le respondió, y dijo: —Pero yo no te dije que vendía el guajolote junto con el carbón.

26. ¿Pues, cuánto crees que vale un guajolote?

27. ¿Crees que se vendería el guajolote con el carbón por trescientos pesos?

28. No se vende por eso.

29. *siʔk guslohreni byehYreni ǰehk baȼehB dadeʔga   Juan*
    like began-they noise-they then scared father-little-that John

    rähpni   lohni   časannählu   lo guštis palga dilu
    saying-he to-him will-leave-with-you to police if-that not-you

    guniiǰ   behDga
    will-give turkey-that

30. *čeni   bawiini šet gakdi   gunni ǰehk badeedni*
    when-that saw-he not will-be-not will-be-it then passed-he

    behDga   lo dadeʔga
    turkey-that to father-little-that

31. *ši   xihG kafee nibääni   lo behDga*
    what cup coffee almost-take-he to turkey-that

32. *lo yä̱lṛǰeʔčga   gusiini   te baryehG nepyeʔt*
    to maddening-that bought-he one gourd   liquor

    sä'tini   roʔ   gehǰga
    going-just-he mouth town-that

29. Like this they began to make
    noise, then the barber was afraid
    of John and he said to him, "I
    will take you to the police be-
    cause you did not give me that
    turkey."

29. Y así empezaron a discutir, tan-
    to, que el peluquero amenazó a
    Juan con acusarlo a las autorida-
    des si no le daba el guajolote.

30. When John saw that he could
    not do anything else, then he
    gave the turkey to that barber.

30. Cuando Juan vio que no podía
    hacer nada más, muy triste entre-
    gó el guajolote con el carbón.

31. He did not even get a cup of cof-
    fee for that turkey.

31. No pudo ni comprar una taza de
    café con la venta del guajolote.

32. Because he was mad, he bought
    a bottle of liquor and went to
    the edge of the town.

32. Juan estaba muy enojado, y por
    su enojo compró un bule de pul-
    que y se fue a la orilla del
    pueblo.

33. *sas guslohni kayä'ni   nepye?tga te   jyällahZni*
    and began-he drinking-he liquor-that that will-strong-heart-he

    šini?k   bennährenini
    what-this made-with-they-he

34. *jehk ro?k suga?ni čeni   bizuhN te bengu*
    then there stand-he when-that arrived one person-drunk

35. *rähpni   lohni   xčan be¢ä*
    saying-he to-him hello brother-my

36. *ši   ruhNlu   ree nabehlu*
    what doing-you here is-sit-you

37. *šikwent runrje?č   lohlu*
    why   being-mad to-you

38. *jehk gusloh Juan kayoon kayähpni lo benguga   ni*
    then began John crying saying-he to person-drunk-that that

    gusahkni
    happened-it

33. And he began to drink mezcal in order to make his heart strong to forget what they had done.

34. There he was when arrived a drunk.

35. And he said to him, "Good afternoon, my brother.

36. What are you doing sitting here?

37. Why are you here being angry?"

38. Then John began to cry and he was telling that drunk all that had happened to him.

33. Y empezó a beber para olvidarse de lo que le había pasado.

34. Allí estaba cuando llegó otro borracho

35. que le dijo: —¡Buenas tardes hermano!

36. ¿Qué haces aquí?

37. ¿Por qué estás aquí, sentado, tan enojado?

38. Juan empezó a llorar y le contó al borracho todo lo que le había pasado.

39. *jehk rähp benguga*   *loh Juan la niʔksi*
then saying person-drunk-that to John QM therefore-just

roonlu   *rsyuhlu*   *rjeʔčlu* *ä*
crying-you stopping-you mad-you QM

40. *narä giniä*   *šiniʔk*   *sahk*   *gunlu*
I   will-say-I what-therefore will-make will-be-you

41. *maske*   *nakä*   *bengu*   *per narä šiniʔk*   *runä*
even-little is-be-I person-drunk but I   what-therefore being-I

42. *jehk benguga*   *lohtis* *baryehGga rwiini* *jehk*
then person-drunk-that to-only gourd-that seeing-he then

rähpni   *kayoldušteä*
saying-he thirsting-very-one-I

43. *la* *di* *gakdini*   *guniijlu*   *čeʔn* *šnislu*   *ni*
QM not will-be-not-it gave-you some of-water-your that

rahplu *nen baryehGga yä'ä* *ä*
having-you in gourd-that drink-I QM

---

39. Then that drunk said to John, "Is that all that is causing you to cry, stopping you, your being angry?

40. I will tell you what to do to get the price (of your turkey).

41. Even though I am a little drunk, I will tell you what I would do."

42. The drunk looked longingly at John's bottle and said to him, "I am very thirsty.

43. Will you not give to me some of your water that you have in the gourd for me to drink?"

39. Entonces el borracho le dijo a Juan: —¿Nada más por eso te pones tan triste, tan enojado?

40. Yo te diré lo que tienes que hacer para recuperar el precio (de tu guajolote).

41. Aunque estoy un poco barracho, te voy a decir lo que debes hacer.

42. El borracho se quedó mirando de reojo el bule de Juan, y al fin le dijo: —Tengo mucha sed.

43. ¿No me podrías dar un poco de esa agua que tienes en el bule?

44. *mbah rähp Juan per tuǰeneʔtisni   yälu*
    OK   saying John but little-little-only-it drink-you

45. *mbah rähpni*
    OK   saying-he

46. *čeni   kwaʔnini guslohni guʔni   sihLni*
    when-that take-he-it began-he drank-he aˆlot-it

    stuǰeneʔsini   basaʔnni par Juan
    other-little-little-just-it left-he   for John

47. *ǰehk rähp Juan et rniä   lohlu čeneʔsini   yälu*
    then saying John not saying-I to-you little-little-just-it drink-you

48. *čeneʔsigala   ni guʔä rähp benguga*
    little-little-just-that-yes that drank-I saying person-drunk-that

    pet   šparyehGlu   arǰun
    maybe of-gourd-your already-leaking

44. "OK," said John, "But only
    drink a little bit."

45. "OK," he said.

46. When he took that bottle he
    drank, he drank also that little
    bit that was left for John.

47. Then John said, "Didn't I say to
    you that you could drink only
    just a little bit?"

48. "I drank just a little bit of it,"
    said the drunk. "Maybe the
    gourd has a leak in it."

44. —Sí —le dijo Juan—, pero toma
    un poquito nada más, y deja lo
    demás para mí.

45. —Está bien —le dijo.

46. El borracho agarró el bule, pero
    no lo soltó hasta que lo dejó va-
    cío.

47. Al verlo, Juan le dijo al borra-
    cho: —¡Mira lo que hiciste! Ya
    me dejaste sin pulque. ¿No dijis-
    te que sólo ibas a tomar un
    poco?

48. —Pues tomé sólo un poco —dijo
    el borracho—, tal vez el bule es-
    tá roto.

49. *jehk guslohreni kawiireni   don   la gulii*
    then began-they seeing-they let's^see QM straight

   benguga   rjun   šparyehGni
   person-drunk-that leaking   of-gourd-his

50. *jehk bašal̲ Juan benguga   saka?ru   nepye?t te*
    then sent John person-drunk-that go-bring-more liquor that

   si?k fiireni   don   la gulii   rjun̲ni
   like see-they let's^see yes straight leaking-it

51. *čeni   bizuhN̲ benguga   guslohreni kayä'reni*
    when-that arrived person-drunk-that began-they drinking-they

   nepye?tga jehk gusloh benguga   kayähp lohni ni
   liquor-that then began person-drunk-that saying to-him that

   gunni
   will-be-he

49. Then they began to look to see
    if what that drunk had said was
    true, that his gourd had a hole
    in it.

50. Then John sent that drunk going
    to get more liquor to see if for
    sure it had leaked out.

51. When the drunk returned they
    began to drink and the drunk
    told him what he should do.

49. Entonces se pusieron a revisar el
    bule para ver si estaba roto.

50. Luego Juan mandó al borracho
    para que fuera por más pulque
    para comprobar si el bule estaba
    roto.

51. Cuando el otro borracho regresó
    comenzaron a tomar, y el borra-
    cho le dijo a Juan lo que debía
    hacer para recuperar el precio
    de su guajolote.

52. *čeni   baluuž beŋguga   rähpni   loh Juan ni*
    when-that finished person-drunk-that saying-he to   John that

    sahk   gunni   ǰehk gudyesreni
    will-make will-be-he then slept-they

53. *basaʔnti Juan rešpurni   naliib*
    left-just John of-donkeys-his is-tie

54. *čeni   wistye   Juan bašekni rešpurni*
    when-that caused-stand John freed-he of-donkeys-he

    sä'tini   rolihZ dadeʔ   ni   ruwah škiǰehkni
    going-just-he house father-little that cutting of-hair-his

55. *če   biẕuhNni gunabni gigah xqiǰehkni ǰehk rähpni   lak*
    when arrived-he asked-he will-cut of-hair-his then saying-he how

    škaʔlu   guwahlu   škiǰekä näh škiǰehk šamigwä
    will-bring-you will-cut-you of-hair-I with of-hair of-friend-my

52. When that drunk was finished, then he told John what he should do, then they slept.

53. John had left his donkeys tied near them.

54. When John stood up he untied his burros, and he went to the house of the barber.

55. When he arrived he asked for a hair cut, then he said, "How much will you charge for cutting my hair and the hair of my friend?"

52. Pero cuando terminaron de tomar el pulque, ya estaban bien borrachos y se quedaron dormidos allí.

53. Sus burros estaban amarrados por allí cerca también.

54. Cuando se le pasó la borrachera, Juan desató sus burros, y se encaminó a la casa del peluquero.

55. Al llegar, le pidió un corte de pelo y le dijo: —¿Cuánto me cobras por cortarme el pelo y el de mi amigo también?

56. *jehk rähp dade?ga lagahk ni ška? guwaä*
then saying father-little-this itself that will-bring will-take-I

škijehklu lagahk si?k ška?ä guwaä škijehk
of-hair-you itself like will-bring-I will-take-I of-hair

šamiigwlu rähp dade?ga
of-friend-your saying father-little-that

57. *bawahtini škijehk Juan jehk rähpni kon šamiigwlu nah*
cut-just-he of-hair John then saying-he where of-friend-your now

58. *jehk baluii Juan šamiigwni jehk rähp dade? žo*
then taught John of-friend-his then saying father-little how

nahklu bentont
was-you person-crazy

59. *žo mood gak bur te šamiigwlu*
how manner will-be donkey one of-friend-your

60. *jehk rähp Juan dini gusaan narä*
then saying John not-he will-permit me

56. Then the barber said, "The same I charge to cut your hair, the same price I will take to cut your friend's hair."

57. He cut John's hair and then he said, "Where is your friend now?"

58. Then John looked at his friend, and that barber said, "Are you crazy?"

59. "How can a burro be your friend?"

60. He said, "He does not leave me."

56. —Pues lo mismo que te cobro a ti le cobraré a él —le dijo el peluquero.

57. Así que, le cortó el pelo a Juan, y cuando terminó le preguntó: —¿Dónde está tu amigo?

58. Juan miró al burro, y el peluquero le dijo: —¿Estás loco?

59. ¿Cómo puede ser que un burro sea tu amigo?

60. Y Juan le dijo: —Él nunca me deja.

61. *kadrotis   rya?ä   rsyahni   bawahga yehkni   nah te*
    where-only going-I running-he cut-that   head-his now that

    kayoblazä
    urging-want-I

62. *jehk rähp   dade?ga   lo Juan narä dina guwaä   yehk*
    then saying father-little-that to John I   not-I will-take-I head

    bur   ree   ruwaä   ganaž yehk renigii
    donkey here cutting-I first   head men

63. *rušihZ   Juan rähpni   dina ganä   per sahplu   por*
    laughing John saying-he not-I will-know-I but will-have-you for

    gunluni
    will-be-you-it

64. *palga dilu   gunni   syanäälu   lo guštis jehk säpä*
    if-that not-you will-be-it will-go-with-I-you to police then will-say-I

    ganaž si?k ruhNlu   rusgeelu   rebehN
    first   like doing-you cause-lying-you persons

61. "Wherever I go, he walks (goes). Cut his hair now so that I can leave."

62. Then the barber said to John, "I will not cut the hair of a donkey, here I cut only the hair of men."

63. John laughed and said, "I do not know but you have to cut his hair.

64. If you do not do it, I will take you to the authorities then I will say that you do not keep your word."

61. Siempre andamos juntos. ¡Córtale el pelo que estoy muy apurado!

62. El peluquero le dijo: —Yo no le corto el pelo a burros, sólo se lo corto a los hombres.

63. Y Juan, riéndose, le dijo: —Yo no sé, pero tú tienes que cumplir tu palabra.

64. Y si no la cumples, te voy a llevar a las autoridades y les diré que tú no cumples tu palabra.

65. *jehk gusloh dade?ga   kaje?čduš nah palga fiireni*
    then began father-little-that mad-very now if-that see-they

    lohni kaguwahni yehk te bur   sustuhYreni
    to-him cutting-he head one donkey will-cause-ashame-they

    lohni jehk rähpni lo Juan di gakdi   guwaä yehk
    to-him then saying-he to John not will-be-not will-cut-I head

    špurlu
    of-donkey-your

66. *narä gunijä   te   gayuu beež te čanäluni   lo*
    I   will-give-I one hundred peso that will-with-you-him to

    stee ni rahk ruwah yehk bur   sa?ksi narä di
    another that making cutting head donkey because I   not

    gakdi   gunäni
    will-be-not will-be-I-it

67. *jehk rähp Juan dina rlazä ška?ä   meel narä*
    then saying John not-I wanting-I will-bring-I money I

    rlazä   fiä   gigah yehk šamigwä
    wanting-I will-see-I will-cut head of-friend-my

65. The barber was very angry now. If people saw him cutting the hair of a donkey they would make him ashamed. Then he said to John, "I cannot cut the hair of your donkey.

66. I will give you a hundred pesos to take the donkey with you to another barber, because I cannot do it here."

67. Then John said, "I do not want to take your money, I want the hair of my friend cut.

65. El peluquero se enojó más, porque sabía que si la gente lo veía cortándole el pelo a un burro se reirían de él; por eso le dijo a Juan: —No puedo cortarle el pelo a tu burro.

66. Pero te puedo dar cien pesos para que vayas a otro peluquero para que se lo corte, porque yo no lo puedo hacer aquí.

67. —No quiero dinero —dijo Juan—. Quiero que le cortes el pelo a mi amigo.

68. *palga dilu   gusobdyahG štijä   syanäälu   lo*
    if-that not-you will-sit-ear of-word-my will-go-with-I-you to

    guštis
    police

69. *jehk rähp dade?ga   gunijä   gaii gayuu   te   na?k*
    then saying father-little-this will-give-I five hundred that not

    čanälu   narä lo guštis
    will-with-you I   to police

70. *jehk rähp Juan et rniä   lohlu dina rlazä   meel*
    then saying John not saying-I to-you not-I wanting-I money

71. *jehk sä'ti   Juan näh rešpu̲rni   rähpni   lo*
    then going-just John with of-donkeys-his saying-he to

    dade?ga   n̲ah sii syayunä   demandlu lo reguštis
    father-little-this now if going-is-with demand-you to police

    te   ganreni   luh si?ktis rusgeelu   rebehN̲
    that will-know-they you like-only cause-lying-you persons

68. If you do not obey my word, then I will take you to the authorities."

69. Then the barber said, "I will give you five hundred pesos in order that you will not take me to the police."

70. Then John said, "Did I not tell you that I do not want money?"

71. Then John was just going with his donkeys and he said to that barber, "I am going now to take this to the authorities so that they will know that you are lying to the people."

68. Ya te dije que si no cumples tu palabra, te voy a llevai a las autoridades.

69. —Bueno —le dijo el peluquero—, te daré quinientos pesos para que no me lleves a las autoridades.

70. —Ya te dije que no quiero dinero —contestó Juan.

71. Y mientras se iba con su burro, le dijo al peluquero: —Ahora sí voy a demandarte ante las autoridades pare que sepan que siempre andas engañando a la gente.

72. *ĵehk gusloh dadeʔga*   *kayähp lohni naʔk čanälu*
then began father-little-that saying   to-him not   will-with-you

narä te gunijä gahĵ gayuu beež lohlu
I   that will-give-I seven hundred peso to-you

73. *če bawiini loh Juan dur sääni lo guštis ĵehk*
when saw-he to John hard going-he to police then

räpsak dadeʔga gunijä teb alm beež
saying-again father-little-this will-give-I one box peso

74. *ĵehk gubiʔ Juan kabalazdušni rähpni škaʔä*
then returned John liking-very-he saying-he will-take-I

meelre saʔksi ryaälu
money-this because compassionate-I-you

75. *paru nakä te nigii maal niyunä demandlu te*
if   is-be-I one man evil almost-do-I demand-you that

nyakbeelu naʔkru gusgeelu rebehN
almost-is-straight-you not-more will-cause-lie-you persons

72. Then the barber said to him, "Do not take me, for I will give you seven hundred pesos."

73. When he saw John determinedly going to the authorities, then he said again to him, "I will give you a box of money."

74. Then John returned. He was very happy and he said, "I will receive the money because I have compassion on you.

75. If I were an evil man, I would take you and press charges so that you would not lie to people any more."

72. El peluquero le rogaba a Juan que no lo demandara, que le daría setecientos pesos.

73. Pero cuando vio que Juan se alejaba, sacó un almud con pesos y le dijo: —No vayas. Mira, te daré una caja de pesos.

74. Entonces Juan regresó muy contento, y le dijo: —Recibiré el dinero porque te tengo compasión.

75. Porque si yo fuera un hombre malo te demandaría, para que aprendas a no engañar a la gente.

76. *byunehZti   Juan ro?k kabalazdušni nähru   špurni*
    was-way-just John there liking-very-he with-more of-donkey-he

    rbalazduxh
    liking-very

77. *asazuhNreni   ro? gehǰga   če   biǰagsakni*
    already-go-arrive-they mouth town-that when met-again-he

    benguga   ǰehk rähp benguga   lohni žo
    person-drunk-that then saying person-drunk-that to-him how

    wihlu be¢ä
    go-you brother-I

78. *ǰehk rähp Juan weenka   wa?a*
    then saying John good-also went-I

79. *ǰehk badeed Juan škištios   lo benguga   por*
    then passed John of-thanks-God to person-drunk-that for

    rediiǰ ni rähpni lohni
    words that saying-he to-him

76. Then Juan, with his donkey, entered his way from there, he was very happy.

77. When he arrived again at the edge of the town, then he met again that drunk who said to him, "How did it go, brother?"

78. Then John said, "It went real well with me."

79. Then John gave thanks to the drunk for the words that he had spoken to him.

76. Y Juan se fue de allí muy contento, con su burro.

77. Cuando llegó a la orilla del pueblo encontró otra vez al borracho, y éste le preguntó: —¿Cómo te fue hermano?

78. Juan le dijo: —Muy bien.

79. Y le agradeció mucho el consejo que le había dado.

80. *jehkti   siiti   Juan rolihZni nähza   rešpurni*
    then-just going-just John house-his with-also of-donkeys-his

81. *sigahkza benguga   sayäsakni*
    like-also person-drunk-that go-drink-again-he

80. Then John went to his house   80. Entonces, Juan regresó a su casa
    with his donkeys.   con su burros.

81. Like manner that drunk went on   81. Y el borracho continuó tomando.
    drinking again.

The Rabbit and the Coyote

Pedro Aguilar

1. *yuʔti te kunehW ni ruhN daan lo tlaʔ bisyaa ni*
   is-just one rabbit that doing damage on patch bean that

   raʔn te dadeʔ
   cultivating one father-little

2. *kayundušži daan niʔkni behNga*
   doing-very-knows damage therefore-that person-that

   biǰeʔčzani saʔksi aguhkni široob daan kayuhNši
   mad-also-he because already-was-he much damage doing-he

1. There was a rabbit doing much damage to a bean patch of a man who was tending it.	1. Había un conejo que siempre andaba haciendo mucho daño en un frijolar.
2. He was doing lots of damage, thus the man was very angry because he was doing a lot of damage.	2. Estaba haciendo tanto daño que el señor que cuidaba el frijolar se enojó mucho.

3. *sas behNtini   šigab   naani   čanazä   manre   naani*
   and made-just-he thought say-he will-grab-I animal-this say-he

   don   čuniʔk kayujN daan   lo špisyaä
   let's^see who   doing damage on of-bean-I

4. *sas bazuhni tramp lo šnesyuh   kunehW bigaʔti*
   and set-he   trap on of-way-ground rabbit grabbed-just

   kunehW
   rabbit

5. *če   gohL bara yääl če   biʒuhNni rolihZni sas*
   when born early night when arrived-he house-his and

   basälni   kunehW nen te yeʔk
   caught-he rabbit in one trap

6. *jehk sayuhNni ʒuun lo špisyaani*
   then go-do-he work on of-bean-his

7. *yuʔti kunehW nen yeʔk*
   is-just rabbit in trap

3. Well then he thought to himself, "I am going to catch this animal and see who is damaging my beans."

4. Well, he set a trap in the path of the rabbit and it grabbed the rabbit.

5. When the evening came, he arrived home, and he caught the rabbit in the trap.

6. Then he went to work in his bean patch.

7. There was the rabbit in the trap.

3. Entonces el señor se dijo: "voy a agarrar a este animal que está causando daño en mi frijolar".

4. Y puso una trampa en el camino del conejo. La trampa lo atrapó.

5. Cuando llegó la noche, el hombre fue a su casa, echó al conejo en una jaula,

6. y se fue a trabajar en su frijolar.

7. El conejo ya estaba dentro de la jaula.

8. *če   sadehD te   kuyoʔt sas bawiini kadro nyäuu   kunehW*
   when go-pass one coyote and saw-he where is-close rabbit

9. *weno amigW rähpni   ši   ruhNlu   ree*
   OK   friend   saying-he what doing-you here

10. *Nikla   ganlu   beȼä   rähpni   narä yuʔä ree   rähpni*
    neither knew-you brother-I saying-he I   is-I   here saying-he

11. *ree   sii nabaṇsaʔk behN̲   rähpni*
    here yes is-live-well person saying-he

12. *žo   mood   rähpni*
    how manner saying-he

13. *mbah rähpni   če   gal̲   or   gušarenä rähpni*
    OK   saying-he when will-born hour will-eat-I saying-he

    suniiǰreni   te   gid   gauä   rähpni
    will-give-they one chicken will-eat-I saying-he

14. *luš ganiddoo suwahZreni   narä rähpni*
    but first-big   will-bathe-they I   saying-he

8. When the coyote was passing, he saw the rabbit in the trap.	8. Pasó un coyote y vio al conejo en la jaula.
9. "Well friend," said the coyote "What are you doing here?"	9. —Bueno, amigo —le dijo—, ¿Qué haces aquí?
10. "Don't you know brother," he said, "that I am here."	10. —¿Sabes por qué estoy aquí?
11. "Here I am really living well," he said.	11. Porque aquí se vive bien —le dijo.
12. "How so?" he said.	12. —¿Cómo? —dijo el coyote.
13. "Well," he said, "when the hour that I eat arrives, they will give me a hen to eat," he (rabbit) said.	13. —Pues sí —le dijo el conejo—, porque a la hora de comer me dan una gallina para comer —le dijo—.
14. "But first they bathe me," he said.	14. Pero antes, me bañan.

15. *an   wenduš   yuʔlu   ree   rähpni*
    OK very-very is-you here saying-he

16. *la   dilu   gičaglahZ   jyaʔnlu   ree   ä   rähpni*
    QM not-you will-gather-heart will-remain-you here QM saying-he

17. *abyedä   narä mano   rähpni   diru   rlazä*
    already-weary-I I   brother saying-he not-more wanting-I

    čuʔä   ree   rähpni   saʔksi   abikesä   gid   rähpni
    will-be-I here saying-he because already-sick-I chicken saying-he

18. *mbahza rähpni   ǰehk palga guliilu   rähpni*
    OK-also saying-he then if-that will-straight-you saying-he

    sahkza   jyaʔnä   donnu   rähpni
    happen-also will-remain-I let's-see-we saying-he

19. *mbahY rähpni   adon   yehNlu   gusälä   kadeen*
    OK   saying-he already-let's-see neck-your will-catch-I chain

    rähpni
    saying-he

15. "OK, it is very good that you are here," he (coyote) said.

16. "Wouldn't you like to stay here?" he (rabbit) said.

17. "I am weary brother," he said, "I do not want to be here," he said "I'm tired of chicken."

18. "OK," he (coyote) said then. "If it is true I will also stay here and see," he said.

19. "OK," said the rabbit. "Let's see, I will put the chain on your neck," he said.

15. —Esto me parece muy bien —le dijo el coyote.

16. —¿No te gustaría quedarte aquí? —le dijo el conejo—.

17. Porque yo ya me aburrí, hermano. Ya me cansé de comer gallina.

18. —Bueno —le dijo el coyote—, si es cierto lo que dices, me quedo.

19. —Bueno —le dijo el conejo—. A ver, acerca tu pescuezo para ponerte la cadena.

20. *sas basä̱lni kadeen yehNni*
    and caught-he chain   neck-his

21. *mbrang byäu roʔ yeʔk*
    Clang   closed mouth trap

22. *sas sä'tivxi*
    and going-just-he

23. *mbah nahktiži*
    OK   was-just-he

24. *če gohL biẕuhṈ or nalahZnu or ni gazni*
    when born arrived hour is-heart-we hour that will-bathe-his

    bačah gool nislaa   šahN   kuyoʔt
    filled mister water-hot bottom coyote

25. *rbeǰaʔ   kuyoʔt*
    screaming coyote

26. *Diostis ni guknäh   kuyoʔt bažṉ̱ sää kuyoʔt*
    God-only that will-make-with coyote ran going coyote

20. Then he put the chain on his neck.	20. Y le puso la cadena en el pescuezo.
21. "Clang" shut the trap.	21. ¡Clang!, cerró la jaula.
22. Then the rabbit left.	22. Entonces se fue el conejo.
23. Well the coyote he was just there.	23. El coyote se quedó dentro de la jaula.
24. When arrived the hour, that is to say the hour of his bath, that man threw hot water over the coyote.	24. Y así pasó un rato, hasta que llegó la hora del baño. Entonces el señor le echó agua caliente al coyote.
25. The coyote screamed (with pain).	25. El coyote gritó de dolor.
26. Only God could help the coyote as he went running.	26. Sólo Dios pudo ayudar al coyote a correr tan rápido.

27. _nah sii naani kadrotis   gijälä   kunehW sauä
    now if say-he where-manner will-find-I rabbit   will-eat-I

    kunehW naani
    rabbit say-he

28. šikwent byädyuhNni latsyah narä
    why   came-did-he liar   I

29. basgeeni   narä nahni gauä   te gid   Luš _nah kon
    caused-lie-he I   say-he will-eat-I one chicken and now where

    gid
    chicken

30. nislaatis   guǰah šanä
    water-hot-only threw bottom-my

31. sati_ltiži   kunehW
    go-look-just-he rabbit

27. "Now if," he said to himself,   27. —¡Aja! Ahora sí, cuando encuen-
    "wherever I find the rabbit, I   tre al conejo, me lo como
    will eat him," he thought.   —dijo—,

28. "Why is he coming lying to me?   28. porque me engañó.

29. He lied to me, he said I would   29. Me engañó. Me dijo que iba yo
    eat a chicken and now where is   a comer una gallina y ahora,
    the chicken?   ¿dónde está la gallina?

30. He just threw hot water on me."   30. Nada más me echaron agua ca-
                                               liente.

31. Then the coyote went looking   31. Y se fue a buscar al conejo.
    for the rabbit.

32. sas   če   biʐuhNni   te   laht   akunehW   sohB   yehk
    and   when   arrived-he   one   place   already-rabbit   sitting   head

    te   yabiʐulahȩ
    one   cactus

33. arniälu   amigW   rähpni   ši   ruhNlu   ree
    already-saying-I-you   friend   saying-he   what   doing-you   here

    rähpni
    saying-he

34. ree   katyuʔä   ninehš   rähpni
    here   cutting-I   fruit   saying-he

35. šikwent   basaʔnlu   narä   rek
    why   left-you   me   there

36. nahlu   loä   gazä   niluš   sas   jyääd   gid   gauä
    say-you   to-me   will-bathe-I   then   and   will-come   chicken   will-eat-I

    rähpni
    saying-he

32. Well, when he arrived in one place, a rabbit was sitting at the top of a tall cactus.

33. "I say to you my friend," he said, "what are you doing here?"

34. "I'm cutting cactus fruit," he said.

35. "Why did you leave me there?

36. You said to me, I will get bathed and then a chicken will come for me to eat," he said.

32. Cuando llegó a un lugar encontró al conejo sentado en la parte alta de un nopal.

33. —Bueno, amigo —le dijo—, ¿qué estás haciendo aquí?

34. —Pues aquí estoy, cortando tunas —dijo el conejo.

35. —¿Por qué me dejaste allá?

36. Me dijiste que me iban a bañar y que después me iban a dar una gallina para comer.

37. *niluš šeti gid   nyauä*
    then not chicken almost-eat-I

38. *nislaatis   gujah šanä   rähpni*
    water-hot-only threw bottom-I saying-he

39. *mertis   nahkni rähpni luh ni dilu   nyuhN   want*
    almost-only was-it saying-he you that not-you almost-do stand

    nyahZlu
    almost-bathe-you

40. *palga nya?nlu   nyääd   te gid   nyahWlu*
    if-that almost-remain-you almost-come one chicken almost-eat-you

    rähpni
    saying-he

41. *mbah nah sauäpak   luh šamigwä   rähpni*
    OK   now will-eat-I-truly you of-friend-my saying-he

37. "But there was not a chicken for me to eat.	37. Y resulta que no hubo tal pollo para que yo comiera.
38. Only hot water was thrown over me," he said.	38. Nada más me echaron agua caliente.
39. "It almost happened," he (rabbit) said, "you did not get through the bath.	39. —Estaba a la perfección el baño. Tú fuiste el que no lo aguantó.
40. If you had stayed, the chicken would have come for you to eat," he said.	40. Si lo hubieras aguantado, a buena hora te hubieran traído una gallina para que comieras —le dijo el conejo.
41. "Well, now, I am really going to eat you my friend," said the coyote.	41. —Bueno —dijo el coyote—, pues ahora te voy a comer a ti.

42. *naʔk gaulu   narä rähpni   kom   et narädini*
    not will-eat-you I   saying-he because not I-not-he

43. *šidahL beȼä   yuʔ rähpni*
    many brother-my is saying-he

44. *pet   teh reniʔk bawiilu rähpni*
    maybe one these saw-you saying-he

45. *nah narä yuʔä ree*
    now I   is-I here

46. *ninehšpak rutyuʔä rähpni*
    fruit-truly cutting-I saying-he

47. *la dilu   gaulu   te ninehš rähpni*
    QM not-you will-eat-you one fruit saying-he

48. *sahkzani   rähpni*
    will-make-also-it saying-he

42. "Do not eat me," the rabbit said, "because I am not that rabbit.

43. There are many brothers of us," he said.

44. "Maybe it was one of them you saw," he said.

45. "I was here.

46. I have been here cutting fruit all the time," he said.

47. "Will you not eat one of these cactus fruit?" he said.

48. "OK," he said.

42. —¡No me comas! —dijo el conejo—, porque yo no soy el mismo conejo que te engañó.

43. Tengo muchos hermanos.

44. Tal vez fue uno de ellos el que viste —le dijo—.

45. Yo estaba aquí.

46. He estado aquí cortando tunas todo este tiempo —le dijo—.

47. ¿No te gustaría comer una tuna? —le preguntó.

48. —Bueno —contestó el coyote.

49. *mbah rähpni   gutyušä   tehni gaulu*
    OK   saying-he will-clean-I one-it will-eat-you

50. *saa batyušni   te   bidzulahȼ*
    then cleaned-he one cactus^fruit

51. *bašal roʔlu   rähpni*
    open mouth-your saying-he

52. *yo rähpni*
    OK saying-he

53. *bastehBni   te   bidzulahȼ   nen roʔni*
    caused-fell-he one cactus^fruit in   mouth-his

54. *ni   barohp wält*
    that second times

55. *rähpni   žo   nahkni*
    saying-he how was-it

56. *hueenka nahkni*
    good-also was-it

49. "OK," he said, "I will clean one
    for you to eat."

50. Then he cleaned a cactus fruit.

51. "Open your mouth," he said.

52. "OK," he said.

53. He threw one of the cactus
    fruits into his mouth.

54. And a second time.

55. He said to him, "How was it?"

56. "It was OK.

49. —Bueno —dijo el conejo—, voy
    a pelar una para que comas.

50. Y peló una tuna.

51. —Abre la boca —dijo el conejo.

52. —Bueno —dijo el coyote.

53. El conejo le tiró la tuna a la
    boca.

54. Y le dijo:

55. —¿Cómo estuvo?

56. —Estuvo bien.

57. *nehšni   nehšni   rähpni*
    sweet-it sweet-it saying-he

58. *mbah jehk nah rähpni   la   sahWlu   steeni*
    OK   then now saying-he QM will-eat-you another-it

59. *sauäza   steeni   per basäuu balohlu rähpni*
    will-eat-I-also another-it but closed eye-your saying-he

60. *mbahY rähpni*
    OK   saying-he

61. *pwes žiʔn man   kunehW batyuʔži biʒulahȼ   jehk*
    well child animal rabbit cut-he cactus^fruit then

    siʔktisni   batyuʔžini bastehBžini   gideb gehč nen roʔ
    like-only-that cut-he-it caused-fell-he-it all spine in mouth

    kuyoʔt
    coyote

62. *rolka   kuyoʔt nagaʔ rbihšni   rtehBni   agaʔni*
    screaming-also coyote is-lying turning-he falling-he is-lying-he

57. It was very sweet," he said.

58. "OK now," he said, "can you eat another one?"

59. "I will eat another one," (said the coyote). "But close your eyes," he (rabbit) said.

60. "OK," said the coyote.

61. Well that son of an animal rabbit, he cut the cactus fruit, then, just like it was with all the spines, he threw it into the coyote's mouth.

62. Screaming, that coyote was lying, turning, throwing (himself) down, lying.

57. Muy dulce —le dijo el coyote.

58. —Bueno, ¿quieres otra?

59. —Sí, quiero otra —dijo el coyote. —Bueno, pero cierra los ojos —dijo el conejo.

60. —Bueno —le dijo el coyote.

61. Y el malvado conejo cortó una tuna, y así como la cortó se la dejó caer en la boca, con todo y espinas.

62. Y el coyote se comenzó a revolcar de dolor.

63. *di   jyen   žo   gunni   girii   gehč   nen̲   ro?ni*
not   will-do   how   will-be-he   will-come^out   spine   in   mouth-his

64. *nahktiži*
was-just-he

65. *ǰehk   gutyähsni   kunehW   yehk   yahGga   ǰehkru   säätiži*
then   jumped-he   rabbit   head   wood-that   then-more   going-just-he

66. *naga?ti   kuyo?t*
is-lying-just   coyote

67. *če   biẓuhN̲ni   stee   laht   satil̲ni   kunehW*
when   arrived-he   another   place   go-look-he   rabbit

68. *kunehW   sohB   ro?   te   geed   kaluii   byuux   n̲ah   mastr*
rabbit   sit   mouth   one   hole   teaching   child   now   teacher

nahkni
was-he

63. He did not know what to do to get the spines out of his mouth.

64. Like this he was.

65. Then the rabbit jumped down from the cactus and he just went.

66. The coyote was still turning in pain.

67. When the coyote arrived at another place, he began to look for the rabbit.

68. The rabbit was sitting at the mouth of a hole teaching children. He was a teacher.

63. No encontraba la forma de quitarse las espinas que tenía en la boca.

64. Así estaba.

65. El conejo, dando un salto, se bajó del nopal y se fue.

66. Mientras, el coyote se quedó revolcándose de dolor.

67. El coyote comenzó a buscar al conejo, y llegó hasta otro lugar.

68. Y allí estaba el conejo sentado a la orilla de un hoyo, enseñando a los niños de la escuela. Ahora era maestro.

69. *sas rähpni ši kayuhNlu ree rähpni*
    and saying-he what doing-you here saying-he

70. *ree kaguluiä byuux eskweel*
    here teaching-I child school

71. *šikwent basgeelu narä rähpni*
    why caused-lied-you I saying-he

72. *bastehBlu bidzulahȼ gideb gehč roʔä rähpni*
    caused-fell-you cactus^fruit all spine mouth-I saying-he

73. *et narädi rähpni yuʔ stee beȼä rähpni*
    not I-not saying-he is another brother-I saying-he

    steeča beȼäži rähpni
    another-perhaps brother-my-he saying-he

74. *saʔksi narä naǰagsaʔä šidahL behȼ*
    because I is-meet-kind-I many brother

69. Then the coyote said, "What are you doing here?" he said.

70. "Here I am teaching children in school."

71. "Why are you lying to me?" he said.

72. "You threw the cactus fruit into my mouth with all the spines on it," he said.

73. "It was not me," said the rabbit, "it was another of my brothers, maybe it was my brother," he said.

74. "Because I have many brothers."

69. —¿Qué estás haciendo aquí? —le dijo el coyote.

70. —Pues, aquí estoy enseñando a los niños de la escuela.

71. —¿Por qué me engañaste? —le dijo—.

72. Me tiraste la tuna con todo y espinas en la boca —dijo el coyote.

73. —Yo no fui —dijo el conejo—; tal vez fue otro de mis hermanos.

74. Porque yo tengo muchos hermanos.

75. *luhpakni   rähpni*
    you-truly-it saying-he

76. *et   narädi rähpni*
    not I-not   saying-he

77. *mastr nakä   šten rebyuux eskweel eskweel rbeʔkä   ree*
    teacher is-be-I of   children school school imparting-I here

    rähpni
    saying-he

78. *arniä   rähpni   benween   rähpni   byanälaa*
    already-saying-I saying-he person-good saying-he stayed-with-favor

    rešpyužä   rähpni   cvaʔä   čakaʔä   ši   gidaunu
    of-children-my   saying-he will-go-I will-bring-I what will-eat-we

    rähpni   dina gaklaä   rähpni   teraʔtsi čaʔä
    saying-he not-I will-be-long-I saying-he little-just will-go-I

    rähpni
    saying-he

75. "It was truly you," said the
    coyote.

76. "It was not I," said the rabbit.

77. "I am a teacher of school
    children. I teach school here," he
    said.

78. "I'm speaking good person," he
    said, "please watch my children,
    I'm going to find something for
    us to eat. I will not be gone
    long, just a little bit," he said.

75. —¡Pero sí, fuiste tú!—dijo el co-
    yote.

76. —Yo no fui —dijo el conejo.

77. —Yo soy maestro de los niños
    de la escuela. Yo doy clase aquí
    —dijo el conejo—.

78. Oye —dijo el conejo—, hazme
    un favor. Cuídame a los niños
    mientras yo voy a traer algo pa-
    ra comer. No me tardo; nada
    más voy por un ratito.

79. *ču gan   kalandušä   rähpni*
    who will-know hungry-am-very-I saying-he

80. *teraʔtsi čaʔä   rähpni   dina gaklaa*
    little-just will-go-I saying-he not-I will-be-long

81. *mbahY rähpni*
    OK   saying-he

82. *palga ganlu   jyäu   roʔ   rebyuužre   rähpni*
    if-that will-know-you will-close mouth children-these saying-he

    yahGeʔre   bakiʔ¢ roʔk rähpni   te   jyohb
    wood-little-this rubbed there saying-he that will-urge

    čanuureni   golreni   golreni   ških¢reni
    will-start-they will-read-they will-read-they of-paper-their

83. *mbahY kaʔtini   te   špaarži sohBtini roʔk*
    OK   bring-just-he one of-bar-he sit-just-he there

79. "Who knows, I am very hungry,"
    said the coyote.

80. "Just a little while I'll be gone,"
    he said, "I will not be gone long."

81. "OK," he said.

82. "If you know the mouths of the
    children are closed, take this
    stick here," he said. "Urge them
    to read, read their papers."

83. OK, he took the stick and he
    just sat there.

79. —No sé. Tengo hambre —dijo
    el coyote.

80. —Pero nada más voy por un rati-
    to. No me tardo.

81. —Está bien —dijo el coyote.

82. —Si ves que los niños están calla-
    dos, metes esta varita allí, para
    que se apuren a leer sus libros.

83. El coyote se quedó allí, con la
    vara en las manos.

84. *aguhkni   š¢ehe?   sää   kunehW mbah satiḻni*
    already-was-it long-little going rabbit   OK   going-looking-he

   ši   gauni
   what will-eat-he

85. *abyeed   kuyo?t sobga?ni ni?k   baki?¢ni baar sas*
    already-weary coyote sit-grab-he therefore rubbed-he bar and

   rsloh   reman ryejhY sas ryacǰisakni
   begining animals noise and being-quiet-again-he

86. *če   biẓe?čni bazedǰe?čni   yahGre neṉ geed*
    when angry-he urged-mad-he wood-this in hole

87. *če   biriyaḻ bäzmatoor guslohži kayauya?ži kuyo?t*
    when went-fast bee-wasp began-he eating-bit-he coyote

88. *bažuṉtiži*
    ran-just-he

84. But a long time passed after the rabbit left to go look for something to eat.

84. Pero pasó mucho tiempo desde que el conejo se fue a buscar la comida.

85. The coyote got weary just sitting there, therefore he moved the stick, and those animals began to make noise, then it was all quiet again.

85. Y el coyote se aburrió de estar sentado y movió la varita. Los animales comenzaron a hacer ruido y luego todo quedó en silencio otra vez.

86. When he was angry, he very angrily put the stick into the hole.

86. Entonces se enojó el coyote, y metió la varita al hoyo con todas sus fuerzas.

87. Then the wasps came out fast and they began to sting the coyote.

87. Y empezaron a salir avispas, y comenzaron a picar al pobre coyote.

88. He just began to run.

88. Y se puso a correr.

89. *ni   guzääb nez nen̠ dyahGni rbihš   rbyahBni sääni*
    that stung   way in   ear-his turning down-he going-he

    sagužun̠ni   mbah
    go-will-run-he OK

90. *kadro ni diru   gakdini   rbihšni   lo yuh*
    where that not-more will-be-not-he turning-he on ground

    siʔktis   sažun̠ni
    like-only go-run-he

91. *n̠ah sii naani di žiʔn manre   gužun̠ loä   narä*
    now yes say-he not child animal-this will-run to-me I

    sauäpakži   naani
    will-eat-I-truly-he say-he

92. *kadrotis fiä   lohni   sauäni*
    where-only will-see-I to-him will-eat-I-him

93. *sä'tini*
    going-just-he

89. They stung (him) in his ear, he was turning, falling down, going running.

90. He was turning rolling in the dirt wherever he was, like this he was running.

91. "Well now," he thought. "This bad animal will not run from me, I will truly eat you," he thought.

92. "Wherever I see him, I will eat him."

93. Then he just went.

89. Pero las avispas lo siguieron y le picaron en las orejas; y se revolcaba y corría.

90. Y se volvía a revolcar, porque ya no aguantaba más.

91. "Bueno pues, ahora sí, este malvado no se me escapa, me lo voy a comer", pensaba.

92. "Me lo voy a comer dondequiera que lo encuentre."

93. Y siguió su camino.

94. *če   biẓuhNni   stee laht   akunehW   sobšuʔnni   niʔ*
    when arrived-he of   place already-rabbit sit-bottom-he foot

    te   gilah   sobẓuʔ¢ sobgaʔni   niʔ gilah
    one stone-cliff sit-firm sit-lying-he foot stone-cliff

95. *če   rlahZni   giriyalni   niʔ gilah   rčalo   kuyoʔt*
    when wanting-he will-go-fast-he foot stone-cliff thinking coyote

    sibihš   gilahre
    will-turn stone-cliff-this

96. *če   biẓuhNni   jehkti   rähpni   ši   kayuhNlu ree*
    when arrived-she then-just saying-he what doing-you here

    rähpni
    saying-he

97. *ree kayaʔpä   gihre   rähpni*
    here watching-I stone-this saying-he

98. *šikwent rähpni*
    why   saying-he

94. When he arrived at another place, that rabbit was sitting on his bottom at the foot of a cliff. He was sitting very firmly with his back against the cliff.

95. He wanted to make the coyote think that he was holding up the rock.

96. When he arrived there he said, "What are you doing here?" he said.

97. "I am watching this rock," said the rabbit.

98. "Why?" said the coyote.

94. Cuando llegó el coyote a otro lugar, allí estaba el conejo recargando la espalda en una roca.

95. Quería que el coyote pensara que en verdad estaba sosteniendo la roca.

96. Entonces cuando llegó, el coyote dijo: —¿Qué estás haciendo aquí?

97. —Aquí estoy, cuidando esta piedra —dijo elconejo.

98. —¿Por qué? —le pregunto el coyote,

99. *palga gusḷaä*   *rähpni*
   if-that will-cause-free-I saying-he

100. *sibekbä'n*   *gejlyuh*   *rähpni*
   will-destroy town-earth saying-he

101. *šomood*   *rähpni*
   how-manner saying-he

102. *bawigan*   *rähpni*   *gusḷaäni*   *gan*   *rähpni*
   looked-know saying-he will-cause-free-I-it will-know saying-he

    te   *fiilu*   *gan*
    that see-you will-know

103. *rbeǰaʔ*   *kuyoʔt rähpni*   *ani*   *basyääd roʔk rähpni*
   screaming coyote saying-he already-that came   there saying-he

104. *ružun*   *kunehW ržaʔtsakni*   *gih*
   running rabbit   shouldering-again-he stone

105. *gunalu*   *pwes rähpni*
   didn't^I^tell-you well saying-he

99. "If I cause it to be free," he said,

100. "the earth will be destroyed," he said.

101. "How so?" he said.

102. "Look and understand," said the rabbit. "I will free it in order that you will see and know."

103. The coyote screamed and said, "It is already falling down," he said.

104. The rabbit ran back again and put his shoulder to the stone.

105. "Well you saw," said the rabbit.

99. —Porque si la suelto —le dijo—,

100. destruye el mundo —le dijo el conejo.

101. —¿Cómo? —dijo el coyote.

102. —Mira —le dijo el conejo—, la voy a soltar para que veas.

103. —¡Se está empezando a caer! —gritó el coyote.

104. Y el conejo corrió y apoyó el hombro en la roca otra vez.

105. —¿Ya ves? —le dijo al coyote.

106. *če   gohL sterä't rähpni   ree bya?n   rähpni*
     when born of-time saying-he here remained saying-he

     čaka?ä   ši   gidaunu   rähpni
     will-bring-I what will-eat-we saying-he

107. *kwanäsihk   ree   rähpni*
     will-take-with-while here saying-he

108. *jehk rähp kuyo?t narä abanahlazä   rähpni   luh*
     then saying coyote I   already-said-heart-I saying-he you

     ni basgee   narä rek   rähpni   niluš nah
     that caused-lied me   there saying-he then now

     gusgesaklu   narä
     will-cause-lie-again-you me

109. *et narädiži mano   rähpni   šidahL be¢ä   yu?*
     not I-not-he brother saying-he many brother-I is

110. *et narädiži rähpni*
     not I-not-he saying-he

106. When a little time had passed, he said, "You stay here. I will go get us something to eat," he said.

107. "Take it awhile here," he said.

108. Then the coyote said, "I remember. You lied to me over there and now you will lie to me again!"

109. "It was not I, brother," he said. "I have many brothers.

110. It was not I," he said.

106. Después de un rato le dijo al coyote: —Bueno, quédate aquí mientras yo voy a traer algo de comer.

107. Detén aquí por un rato —dijo el conejo.

108. —No —dijo el coyote— porque ahora me acuerdo que tú me engañaste una vez, y ahora quieres engañarme otra vez.

109. —No hermano, no fui yo. Yo tengo muchos hermanos.

110. No era yo —le dijo.

111. *anaä   luhni*
     already-say-I you-it

112. *ṇah rähpni   sauälu*
     now saying-he will-eat-I-you

113. *naʔk rähpni   naʔk gaulu   narä et   narädini rähpni*
     not saying-he not   will-eat-you me   not I-not-he saying-he

114. *mbah rähpni*
     OK   saying-he

115. *byaʔn   ree rähpni   te   čakaʔä   ši   gidaunu*
     remained here saying-he that will-bring-I what will-eat-we

116. *yo rähpni*
     OK saying-he

117. *sas byaʔnni   sobšuʔnni   niʔ gilah*
     and remained-he sit-bottom-he foot stone-cliff

111. "I say you are he."

112. "Now," he said, "I am going to
     eat you."

113. "No," said the rabbit. "Do not
     eat me. I am not he," he said.

114. "OK," he said.

115. "Stay here," he said, "in order
     that I go bring what we will eat."

116. "OK," said the coyote.

117. Well, he stayed at the bottom of
     that stone.

111. —No. Sí fuiste tú.

112. Y ahora te voy a comer.

113. —No, no me comas, no fui yo
     —dijo el conejo.

114. —Bueno —dijo el coyote.

115. —Quédate a cuidar la piedra.
     Yo voy a traer algo de comer.

116. —Bueno —dijo el coyote.

117. Y se quedó a cuidar la piedra.

118. *če   gohL byeed kuyoʔt sobgaʔtisni   roʔk*
     when born weary coyote sit-lying-only-he there

119. *sas naani koorča   jyääd   žiʔn manre   narä*
     and say-he what-hour-perhaps will-come child animal-this I

     akalanä   naani
     already-hungrying-I say-he

120. *nah suslaa   gihre   naani*
     now will-cause-free stone-this say-he

121. *sas baslagužunnini*
     and caused-free-will-run-he-it

122. *če   birigužunni   sääni   nezrek   bah syädgužunni*
     when went-will-run-he going-he way-there OK coming-will-run-he

     gunaazniži   stee   te   di   gibišätži
     will-grab-he-he again that not will-knockˆdown-he

123. *žo gibihšži   laltis   sobgaʔži*
     how will-turn-he while-only sit-lying-he

118. Well, that coyote grew weary just sitting there.

119. Then he thought, "What time will the rabbit return? I'm already hungry," he thought.

120. "Now I will turn lose this rock," he thought.

121. Then he turned loose and ran from it.

122. He came again running to grab it in order that it not fall.

123. But the rock, how would it fall if it is sitting in one place?

118. El conejo no regresaba, y el coyote se cansó de cuidar la piedra.

119. Y pensó: "¿A qué hora vendrá ese malvado conejo? Porque yo ya tengo hambre.

120. Ya estoy cansado. Mejor suelto la piedra."

121. Y cuando la soltó, se hizo a un lado,

122. pero en seguida regresó a sostenerla para que no se cayera.

123. Pero, ¿cómo se iba a caer la piedra si estaba en un solo lugar?

124. *če   gule?k lahZni teh baslaani   guih ǰehk galäii*
     when placed heart-he one caused-free-he stone then middle

     nez rek bikweni logargahk   sobga? guih žo
     way there sat-he   on-place-immediately sit-lying stone how

     gibihšni
     will-turn-he

125. *mbah nah sii naani gauä   ži?n manre   kadrotis*
     OK   now yes say-he will-eat-I child animal-this where-only

     giga?ži   naani
     will-stand-he say-he

126. *säätini*
     going-just-he

127. *če biẓuhNni stee   laht a   kunehW sohB loh te*
     when arrived-he another place already rabbit sit to one

     činaa golbeȼ
     flock buzzard

124. When he hardened his heart (got up his courage), he let the rock go, then the rock just sat there, it just stood there in place, how could it fall!

125. "OK now," he thought. "I'm going to eat that son of an animal wherever he is," he thought.

126. Then he left.

127. When he arrived at another place, there was the rabbit tending buzzards.

124. Después de un rato, se decidió, al fin, a soltar la piedra; y cuando la soltó, corrió. Pero la piedra no se movió, no se cayó.

125. Y pensó: "Ahora sí, me voy a comer a ese malvado en dondequiera que yo lo encuentre."

126. Y se fue.

127. Cuando llegó a un lugar, el conejo estaba allí, sentado mirando a un montón de zopilotes.

128. *sobgaʔni   roʔk*
     sit-lying-he there

129. *jehkti   rähpni   ši   kayuhNlu   ree   rähpni*
     then-just saying-he what doing-you here saying-he

130. *ree   kayapä   behD   rähpni*
     here tending-I turkey saying-he

131. *koorča   jyädnälu   ši   gidaunu   rähpni*
     what-hour-well will-come-with-you what will-eat-we saying-he

132. *ana   kabäzätilu   coor   giẕunnähluni*
     already-I waiting-I-just-you what-hour will-arrive-with-you-it

133. *karo   rähpni*
     where saying-he

134. *kat   basannählu   narä kanä   gih   rähpni*
     where left-with-you me   will-tend-I stone saying-he

128. He was just sitting there.

129. Then he said, "What are you
     doing here?" he said.

130. "I am tending turkeys," he said.

131. "What time were you coming
     with our food?" he said.

132. "I was waiting for you just what-
     ever time you would bring it."

133. "Where?" he said.

134. "Where you left me. I was tend-
     ing that stone," he said.

128. Sólo estaba sentado allí.

129. —¿Qué estás haciendo aquí?
     —le dijo el coyote.

130. —Pues aquí estoy, cuidando mis
     guajolotes —dijo el conejo.

131. —¿A qué hora a vas a traer lo
     que vamos a comer? —le dijo el
     coyote—.

132. Estaba esperando que lo trajeras.

133. —¿A dónde? —dijo el conejo.

134. —Donde me dejaste cuidando la
     piedra —le dijo.

135. *et   narädiži šamigwä   rähpni   pet   beʔä   čani*
     not I-not-he of-brother-I saying-he maybe brother-I perhaps-it

     rähpni   narä behDpak   rapä   rähpni
     saying-he I   turkey-truly tending-I saying-he

136. *amiälu   rähpni*
     already-saying-I-you saying-he

137. *beh<u>N</u> ween byanälaa   behD   štenä   rähpni*
     person good stayed-I-please turkey of-me saying-he

138. *čakaʔä   ši   gidaunu*
     will-bring-I what will-eat-we

135. "It was not I, my friend," he
     said. "Maybe it was, perhaps, my
     brother," he said. "I truly tend
     only turkeys," he said.

136. "Look my friend," said the rabbit.

137. "Please look after my turkeys,"
     he said.

138. "I will bring what we will eat.

135. —No fui yo, amigo. Tal vez mi
     otro hermano. Yo siempre cuido
     guajolotes—.

136. Oye amigo —dijo el conejo—.

137. Cuida mis guajolotes, por favor
     —le dijo—,

138. para que yo vaya yo a traer algo
     de comer.

139. *palga gaanlu   gaklaä   rähpni   gunaazga   te*
     if-that will-know-you will-be-long-I saying-he will-grab-that one

     špedä   roʔk gudahW rähpni gažähsi   gaklaä
     of-turkey-my there will-eat saying-he chance-just will-be-long-I

     rähpni   saʔksi   ču   gan   sijälgahkä   ši
     saying-he because who will-know will-found-immediately-I what

     gidaunu   rähpni
     will-eat-we saying-he

140. *mbah rähpni*
     OK   saying-he

141. *sas gunaazni   nehZ   sä'tivxi*
     and grabbed-he way going-just-he

142. *nah sii susgeä   kunehW naani gulähZtero*
     now yes will-cause-lie-I rabbit say-he will-wait-one-big

     gan   naani
     will-know say-he

139. If you see I am a long time," he said, "grab one of my turkeys there to eat it." Perhaps I am just long in coming because who knows if I will immediately find our food," said the rabbit.

140. "OK," said the coyote.

141. Well he took a trail and left.

142. "Now I will lie to the rabbit," he thought, "I'll wait just a little," he thought.

139. Si vez que me tardo, agarras un guajolote y te lo comes. Por que no estoy seguro de encontrar comida enseguida —dijo el conejo.

140. —Bueno —dijo el coyote.

141. Y se fue el conejo.

142. "Anda malvado conejo, ahora sí me voy a desquitar de lo que has hecho, espérate y verás", pensó el coyote.

143. *nuhNsi sää   kunehW čela   biža?tni   loh teh behD*
     not-just going rabbit   when-yes shouldered-he for one turkey

144. *giragahG   behD guyäs jyaa rčelohtisni   sää   rebehD*
     all-immediately turkey flew above amazing-only-he going turkeys

145. *jehk ruwiitisni   nalahZ ruhN lohni ruwiini   jyaa sää*
     then seeing-only-he is-heart doing to-him seeing-he above going

     remanga   rähpni   abasgee   ži?n manre   narä
     animals-these saying-he   already-caused-lied child animal-this I

     stee   naani
     another say-he

146. *ši   moodži*
     what manner-he

143. The rabbit did not come, and he reached towards a turkey.

144. All of the turkeys flew up. He just looked as the turkeys left.

145. Then he just looked sad, that is to say, his face was sad when he saw those turkeys (buzzards) flying. He said, "That son of an animal has lied to me again," he thought.

146. "What way is it?"

143. Apenas desapareció el conejo, trató de agarrar un "guajolote".

144. Pero toditos los "guajolotes" volaron, y el coyote se quedó mirando al cielo.

145. Mientras miraba al cielo, viendo a todos los guajolotes (zopilotes) volar, puso una cara muy triste, pues se dio cuenta de que no eran guajolotes, sino zopilotes.

146. "Ya me la volvió a hacer.

147. *ṇah sii kadrotis   giǰagä   žiʔn manre   suguʔtäži*
     now yes where-only will-meet-I child animal-this will-kill-I-he

     naani
     say-he

148. *säsakni   stee*
     go-again-he another

149. *če   biẓuhṆni   stee   laht akunehW   sobgaʔ roʔ*
     when arrived-he another place already-rabbit sit-lying mouth

     te   bisye
     one   well

150. *rǰelohni   roʔk askanu yuʔ kes   šahN   nisga*
     amazing-he there appear is   cheese bottom water-that

151. *Luš loh bäii   ruwiini   bah et   lo   kesdi*
     and to   moon seeing-he OK   not on cheese-not

152. *če   biẓuhṆ kuyoʔt roʔk ši   ruhNlu   ree   rähpni*
     when arrived coyote there what doing-you here saying-he

147. "Well, wherever I meet this son of an animal, I will kill him," he thought.

147. Ahora, cuando encuentre a ese malvado, lo mato", pensó el coyote.

148. He went to another place.

148. Y se fue.

149. When he arrived at another place, there was a rabbit sitting at the mouth of a well.

149. Pronto encontró al conejo en otra parte, sentado frente a un pozo.

150. He was looking intently at what appeared to be cheese at the bottom of the well.

150. Estaba viendo con fijeza algo que parecía ser un queso en el fondo del charco.

151. And it was the moon he was seeing, it was not cheese.

151. Pero lo que veía dentro del agua no era un queso, sino el reflejo de la luna en el agua.

152. When the coyote arrived there, he said, "What are you doing here?"

152. Cuando llegó el coyote le dijo: —¿Qué haces aquí?

153. *ree   kabää   kes   rähpni*
here getting-I cheese saying-he

154. *la   kes   rbäälu   rähpni*
QM cheese taking-you saying-he

155. *oʔn kes   rbää   rähpni   guknäh   narä gidunnu*
yes cheese getting-I saying-he made-with I   will-drink-we

nisre   te   giläänu   kes   rähpni
water-this that will-take-we cheese saying-he

156. *nah banahlazä rähpni   šikwent basgeelu   narä*
now said-heart saying-he why   caused-lied-you me

basannählu   narä behD   rähpni
left-with-you I   turkey saying-he

157. *et   narädiži rähpni*
not I-not-he saying-he

158. *pet   luhži   rähpni*
maybe you-he saying-he

153. "I'm getting out this cheese," he said.

154. "Are you getting cheese?" he said.

155. "Yes, I'm getting out cheese," said the rabbit. "Help me drink this water in order that we get this cheese," he said.

156. "Now I remember," said the coyote. "Why did you lie to me and leave me watching your turkeys?" he said.

157. "I was not the one," said the rabbit.

158. "Maybe it was you," said the coyote.

153. —Estoy sacando ese queso —dijo el conejo.

154. —¿Estás sacando ese queso? —preguntó el coyote.

155. —Sí, estoy sacando ese queso. Ayúdame a tomar toda esta agua para sacar el queso —dijo el conejo.

156. —Ahora que me acuerdo —dijo el coyote—, ¿por qué me mentiste y me dejaste con los "guajolotes"?

157. —No fui yo —dijo el conejo.

158. —¡Humm! Creo que fuiste tú —dijo el coyote.

159. *stee   beȼäži   rähpni   et   narädiži*
     another brother-I-he saying-he not I-not-he

160. *bikähYza   kuyoʔt bah*
     obscured-also coyote OK

161. *guslohza   kuyoʔt kayä'   nis   dur   kayä'ni*
     will-begin-also coyote drinking water hard drinking-he

162. *kunehW ruhNsini   siʔk ni   kayä'ni   nis   te*
     rabbit doing-just-he like that drinking-he water that

     kwääreni   kes
     will-take-they cheese

163. *ya meriʔt jyennu   gaan   rähpni*
     yes almost will-do-we will-know saying-he

164. *guʔru   nis   rähpni*
     (you)-drink-more water saying-he

159. "It was one of my brothers,"
     said the rabbit, "it was not I."

160. The coyote was fooled again.

161. The coyote began to drink
     water, very hard he was drinking
     it.

162. The rabbit just made like he was
     drinking the water in order to
     get the cheese.

163. "Yes, we are almost ready to get
     the cheese," said the rabbit.

164. "Drink some more," said the rab-
     bit.

159. —Tal vez fue mi hermano. Yo
     no fui —dijo el conejo.

160. Y lo creyó el coyote otra vez.

161. Y comenzó a beber el agua con
     ganas.

162. Y el conejo hacía como que esta-
     ba tomando agua para sacar el
     queso.

163. —Ya casi vamos a sacar el que-
     so —dijo el conejo—.

164. Toma más agua —dijo el cone-
     jo—,

165. *ya   meer   gaan   rähpni*
     yes   almost   will-know   saying-he

166. *če   gujah   žke?   manre   diruna   gunä   want*
     when   filled   stomach   animal-this   not-more-I   will-be-I   stand

     rähpni
     saying-he

167. *ya   meri?t   rähpni   steetis   steetis   jalone?*
     yes   almost   saying-he   another-just   another-only   gallon-little

168. *räji   kunehW   rä'ni   nis   nä*
     drinking-quiet   rabbit   drinking-he   water   with

169. *Luš   rusgeeni   lake?tis   te   bokbäz   nis*
     and   cause-lying-he   how-little-only   one   mouth-little   water

     rä'ni
     drinking-he

165. "Almost we have gotten it," said the rabbit.

166. When the stomach of the coyote was full, he said, "I cannot drink any more.

167. "We are almost there," said the rabbit, "just a little, a gallon more."

168. The rabbit was drinking quietly water.

169. And the rabbit was lying, only a little bit of the water in his mouth was he drinking.

165. ya casi vamos a sacar el queso —dijo el conejo.

166. Y cuando se llenó la barriga, el coyote le dijo al conejo: —Ya no aguanto más.

167. —Ya casi vamos a ganar. Dale otro jaloncito nada más.

168. Y el conejo hacía como que tomaba también.

169. El conejo estaba engañando al coyote, porque él sólo tomaba un poquito de agua.

170. *če   gudedkaj gujah nis   žke?   kuyoʔt gusloh karii*
when happened filled water stomach coyote began coming^out

nis   nez   šahNži   roʔži   gedžiʔži
water way bottom-his mouth-his hole-nose-his

171. *karii   nis   giraa diahGži nagabihšni*
coming^out water all   ear-his is-lying-turn-he

172. *sas bažunti kunehW*
and ran-just rabbit

173. *žiʔn manga   naani če   banah lahZni   kunehWga bahlu*
child animal-that say-he when said   heart-he rabbit-that OK-you

174. *rwiini · kon   kunehW Luš ruti kunehW kanehZ   sääni*
seeing-he where rabbit   and not rabbit   where-way going-he

175. *gurahW naani per nah kanehZ   gijähLži   naani*
ate   say-he but now where-way will-find-he say-he

170. When the coyote's stomach was full of water, it began to come out of his bottom, his mouth, and his nose.

170. Y cuando se le llenó la barriga al coyote, tanto que ya no le cabía más, entonces empezó a salirle agua por la boca y la nariz.

171. Water was coming out of his ears and he was turning lying down.

171. Le salía agua por las orejas y se revolcaba.

172. Well, the rabbit just ran.

172. El conejo se fue.

173. "That son of an animal," he thought, when he remembered that rabbit, "OK, you."

173. —"¡Ah malvado!", pensó el coyote.

174. He looked for the rabbit and he could not find him, he was gone.

174. Y miraba por todos lados buscando al conejo, pero el conejo ya no estaba; se había ido.

175. "I will eat him wherever I find him," he thought.

175. "Cuando lo encuentre, me lo voy a comer vivo", pensó el coyote.

176. *čatiḻäži   gidoṇnu   naani kadrotis   gijähLäži*
     will-look-I-him will-let's^see-we say-he where-only will-find-I-him

     gauäži
     will-eat-I-him

177. *če   wilahni   stee   laht akunehW   sobga?*
     when went-place-he another place already-rabbit sit-lying

     kayunčeeni   te   rohB
     doing-made-he one   basket

178. *sohBni tre? zihN   lohni kaguzaani rohB*
     sit-he gather palm^leaf to-him weaving-he basket

179. *ši   kayuhNlu   ree rähpni*
     what doing-you here saying-he

180. *ree   kayunä rohB   rähpni*
     here doing-I basket saying-he

176. "I will go looking for him. Let's see," he thought, "wherever I find him, I will eat him."

176. "Lo voy a buscar", pensó, "y donde lo encuentre me lo voy a comer".

177. When he came to another place, there the rabbit was sitting making a basket.

177. Después encontró al conejo en otro lugar, tejiendo un tenate.

178. He was sitting there with palm strips in front of him, he was weaving a basket.

178. Estaba allí sentado, con tiras de palmas junto a él, tejiendo un tenate.

179. "What are you doing here?" he said.

179. —¿Qué estás haciendo aquí? —dijo el coyote.

180. "I'm here making a basket," he said.

180. —Estoy haciendo un tenate —contestó el conejo.

181. *šikwent basgeelu   narä rähpni*
     why   caused-lied-you I   saying-he

182. *nahlu gibäänu   kes   rähpni   niluš jehktiru   kon*
     say-you will-take-we cheese saying-he then then-just-more where

     kes   nirii   rähpni
     cheese almost-come^out saying-he

183. *dini   nirii*
     not-it almost-come^out

184. *karo rähpni*
     where saying-he

185. *la   tal roʔk rähpni*
     QM well there saying-he

186. *et   narädiži rähpni*
     not I-not-he saying-he

187. *et   narädiži amɪgW rähpni*
     not I-not-he friend   saying-he

181. "Why did you lie to me?" he
     said.

182. "You said to me we would take
     out cheese," said the coyote.
     "But there was no cheese to
     take out," he said.

183. "There was none to take out."

184. "Where?" asked the rabbit.

185. "Well, there," he said.

186. "It was not I," said the rabbit.

187. "It was not I, friend," said the
     rabbit.

181. —¿Por qué me engañaste?
     —dijo el coyote—.

182. Me dijiste que íbamos a sacar el
     queso, y no salió el queso.

183. No había ningún queso para salir.

184. —¿Dónde?—preguntó el conejo.

185. —Pues allá —dijo el coyote.

186. —Yo no fui —dijo el conejo—.

187. Yo no fui, amigo.

188. *ṉah sii abyedliä*
     now yes already-knew-much-I

189. *ṉah sauäpak   luh rähpni*
     now will-eat-I-truly you saying-he

190. *naʔk gaulu   narä rähpni*
     not   will-eat-you   me   saying-he

191. *šamigwälu   komp rähpni*
     of-brother-I-your friend saying-he

192. *če   gohL steraʔt   arniä   rähpni*
     when born more-moment   already-saying-I   saying-he

193. *lab yehN   dyahGlu sahk   fis   rähpni*
     QM   heard ear-you   will-make judgment saying-he

194. *aii*
     Oh!

188. "Now I know it was you.	188. —Sí, tú fuiste.
189. Now I am going to eat you alive," said the coyote.	189. Por eso, ahora te voy a comer enterito y vivo —dijo el coyote.
190. "Don't you eat me," said the rabbit.	190. —¡No me comas! —dijo el conejo—.
191. "No, you are my friend," said the rabbit.	191. Yo soy tu amigo.
192. A moment went by and the rabbit said, "I say,	192. Ya que pasó un rato, le dijo el conejo: —Oye,
193. have you not heard there is a judgment coming?" he said.	193. ¿no has oído que va a haber un juicio? —dijo el conejo—.
194. "Oh!"	194. ¡Ah!

195. *sahk   fis   rähpni*
     will-make judgment saying-he

196. *čuh*
     who^knows

197. *dina ganä   rähp   kuyoʔt*
     not-I will-know-I saying coyote

198. *sahk   rähpni   jyahB gižobduš   siʔk nahreni*
     will-make saying-he will-fall stone-corn-great like say-they

199. *niʔk   kayunčeä   te   štyobä   kayunšgaäni te   di*
     therefore doing-well-I one of-basket-my doing-first-I-it that not

     juʔt   gižob   narä rähpni
     will-kill stone-corn I   saying-he

200. *benčee   te   štyobä   rähpni*
     make-made one of-basket-my saying-he

201. *mbah rähp*
     OK   saying

195. "A judgment will come," said   195. Un juicio viene —dijo el
     the rabbit.   conejo—.

196. "Who knows."   196. ¡Quien sabe!

197. "I did not know," said the coyote.   197. —No lo sabía —dijo el coyote.

198. "It will happen," said the rabbit.   198. —Sí, eso va a pasar. Va caer
     "Big hail will fall, they say.   granizo muy grande.

199. Therefore, I am making myself a   199. Por eso estoy haciendo un tena-
     basket. I'm making mine in   te. Para meterme adentro y así
     order that the hail will not kill   no me mate el granizo cuando
     me," said the rabbit.   empiece el juicio —dijo el conejo.

200. "Make a basket for me," said   200. —Por favor, hazme un tenate
     the coyote.   —dijo el coyote.

201. "OK," said the rabbit.   201. —Bueno —dijo el conejo—.

202. *goht te   gurešä   luh rähpni*
     sat that will-measure-I you saying-he

203. *sas goht kuyoʔt bareš   kunehW kuyoʔt*
     and sat coyote measured rabbit coyote

204. *ganiddoo štyohBlu   gunä   rähpni   jehktiru*
     first-big of-basket-you willˆmake-I saying-he then-just-more

     gunä   štyobä
     willˆmake-I of-basket-I

205. *mbah rähp kuyoʔt*
     OK   saying coyote

206. *sobgaʔtini   roʔk*
     sit-lying-just-he there

207. *sanuu kayuhNni ʒuun*
     go-start doing-he work

202. "Sit so I can measure you," said the rabbit.

203. The coyote sat and the rabbit measured him.

204. "First I will make your basket," said the rabbit, "then I will make my basket."

205. "OK," said the coyote.

206. He was just sitting there.

207. He started doing the work.

202. Acuéstate aquí para tomarte las medidas —dijo el conejo.

203. El coyote se acostó para que el conejo le tomara las medidas.

204. —Primero voy a hacer tu tenate y luego hago el mío —dijo el conejo.

205. —Bueno —dijo el coyote.

206. El coyote sólo estaba sentado allá.

207. Entonces el conejo comenzó a trabajar.

208. *ǰehk rähpni   koorža   luuž štyohBlu   rähpni*
     then saying-he what-hour-well finish of-basket-your saying-he

209. *gulužätis   štyohBlu   ǰehktiru   gunäza*
     will-finish-I-only of-basket-you then-just-more will-be-I-also

     štobä   rähpni
     of-basket-I saying-he

210. *mbah rähpni*
     OK   saying-he

211. *sanuutis   kayuhNniži*
     go-start-only doing-he-it

212. *akadedlagaa   rohBga   bah siʔkti   barešni*
     already-passing-while basket-that OK   like-just measured-he

     kuyoʔt kom   guroobži
     coyote   because grew-he

213. *sas guyuʔži nen rohB*
     and was-he   in   basket

208. "What time will you finish your basket?" asked the coyote.	208. —¿Y a qué hora vas a hacer tu tenate? —preguntó el coyote.
209. "I will finish your basket," said the rabbit, "then I will make my basket."	209. —Primero, déjame terminar tu tenate. Luego voy a hacer el mío.
210. "OK," said the coyote.	210. —Bueno —dijo el coyote.
211. He was working hard on it.	211. Entonces el conejo comenzó a trabajar muy duro.
212. And a while passed making that basket. OK, it was just like he measured the coyote because it was large.	212. Trabajó mucho tiempo, porque el tenate del coyote tenía que ser grande.
213. And the coyote was in the basket.	213. Después, el coyote se metió al tenate.

214. *jehkru   gudihB kunehW ro?ži   bawalžini lo yahG*
     then-more sewed rabbit mouth-he hung-he-it on tree

215. *če   guluhž gohlži lo yahG bahY nah sii gunä*
     when finished hung-he to tree OK now yes will-be-I

     štobä   rähpni   abiju?lu   nenži
     of-basket-my saying-he already-secured-you in-it

216. *jehkti   guslohni   kunehW katyedahNni   gih*
     then-just will-begin-he rabbit standing-mountain-he stone

217. *gule?kni te činaduš gih*
     placed-he one pile-very stone

218. *jehk rähpni   konlu   rähpni*
     then saying-he where-you saying-he

219. *anaree   rähpni*
     already-I-here saying-he

220. *aii*
     Oh!

214. Then the rabbit sewed the mouth shut and he hung it in a tree.

215. When he finished hanging him in a tree, "Now I will make my basket," he said. "You are secure in there."

216. Then the rabbit gathered a big pile of stones.

217. He gathered a big pile of stones.

218. Then the rabbit said, "Where are you?"

219. "Here I am," said the coyote.

220. "Oh!"

214. Entonces el conejo tejió la orilla del tenate y lo colgó en un árbol.

215. Ya que lo colgó le dijo: —Ahora sí voy a empezar a hacer mi tenate. Ya tú estarás seguro allá adentro.

216. Entonces, el conejo juntó un gran montón de piedras.

217. Ya tenía un montón de piedras.

218. Entonces dijo el conejo: —¿En donde estás?

219. —Aquí estoy —dijo el coyote.

220. —¡Pobre!

221. *nah sii asyäädni   rähpni*
     now yes already-coming-it saying-he

222. *gudobni te   pun   gibiruu   bakwaani šahNni*
     chose-he one sharp stone-river nailed-he bottom-his

223. *aii*
     Oh!

224. *ani   abizuhN   rähpni*
     already-it already-arrived saying-he

225. *guslonähni   kagukwaani gih   yehk kuyoʔt*
     began-with-he nailing-he   stone head coyote

226. *mboh mboh tyešži   sanuutis   kakwaani gih*
     mboh mboh body-his go-start-only nailing-he stone

227. *rbeǰaduš   kuyoʔt*
     screaming-very coyote

221. "Now it is coming," said the rabbit.

222. He chose a sharp river stone and hit his bottom.

223. "Oh!"

224. "Already it has arrived," said the rabbit.

225. Then he began to throw stones at the head of the coyote.

226. Thug, thug, was the sound of the stones hitting the coyote's body.

227. The coyote was screaming greatly.

221. Ahora sí comenzó el juicio —dijo el conejo.

222. Escogió una piedra del río y se la tiró en las nalgas.

223. ¡Pobre!

224. Ahora sí ya comenzó el juicio —dijo el conejo.

225. Y el conejo agarró el montón de piedras y comenzó a tirárselas al coyote.

226. ¡Bam, bam, bami, sonaban las pedradas en la espalda del coyote.

227. El coyote gritaba mucho.

228. *jehkti   rähpni   setä   setä   rähpni*
     then-just saying-he will-die-I will-die-I saying-he

229. *sigahGza narä rähp kunehW kadeddušä   trabahW rähpni*
     like-also I   saying rabbit passing-very-I suffering saying-he

230. *bastihp   lahZlu   meriʔt tedži   rähpni*
     caused-strong heart-you almost will-pass-it saying-he

231. *ni laaži žo tedži   sanuutis   kakooži   gih bah*
     that is-it how will-pass-he go-start-only scraping-he stone OK

232. *behNži   gaan baguʔtžini*
     person-he know killed-he-him

233. *guhksi guhtži diruži   giniib   jitis   yuʔži bah*
     was-just died-he not-more-he will-move quiet-only is-he OK

234. *diži   ninii*
     not-he almost-say

228. Then the coyote said, "I'm
     dying, I'm dying."

229. "The same is happening to me,"
     said the rabbit. "I am suffering
     intensely," said the rabbit.

230. "Make your heart strong! It is
     about to pass," said the rabbit.

231. How could he stop! He just kept
     scrapping up rocks.

232. The rabbit won, he killed the
     coyote.

233. Like this it happened. He died,
     he did not move, he was just
     quiet.

234. He did not say anything.

228. —¡Ay! ¡Me muero, me muero!
     —decía el coyote.

229. —Lo mismo me está pasando a
     mí —dijo el conejo—; estoy su-
     friendo mucho.

230. Pero aguántate. Ya casi va a pa-
     sar —dijo el conejo.

231. Pero ¿cómo iba pasar? Si el co-
     nejo era el le estaba tirando
     duro con las piedras.

232. El conejo ganó, porque mató al
     coyote.

233. Así murió el coyote. Ya no se
     quejaba ni se movía.

234. No decía nada.

235. *bažuṇti kunehW roʔk sä'ti   kunehW*
ran-just rabbit   there going-just rabbit

236. *roʔkti   gubiʔä   syäḻä   ǰehk*
there-just returned-I coming-I then

235. And the rabbit ran, he just went.

236. There I returned, I came then.

235. Entonces el conejo se echó a correr y se fue lejos de allí.

236. Y yo me volteé, y me vine.

The Lion Meets a Man

Pedro Aguilar

1. *yuʔ te lyoon rlahZži fiiži lakti nani laa nigii*
   is one lion wanting-he will-see-he how-just that name^is man

2. *saʔksi ryehN dyahGni ruzä'treni nigii*
   because hearing ear-he talking^about-they man

3. *jehk naatini fiä loh nigii don lakti nigii*
   then say-just-he will-see-I to man let's^see how-just man

---

1. There was a lion who wanted to see just how big is the one who is called man.

2. He had heard the man talked about.

3. Then he said to himself that he would go see a man to know if he was great.

1. Había un león que quería ver él tamaño de lo que se llama hombre.

2. Porque había oído hablar del tal hombre.

3. Entonces se dijo que iría a ver un hombre para saber si de veras era tan grande.

4. *sas kansahni kagiilni nigii*
   and walking-he looking-he man

5. *lyoonre wilahni loh te gonmaaž suga?ži nen̲ yahG naani*
   lion-this named-he to one ox-steer stand-he in tree say-he

   deeži laa nigii
   these-he name^is man

6. *sas gurehni gulääni ro? bišugn̲aani sabigtiniži*
   and sat-he took-he mouth toenail-hand-his go-close-just-he-him

7. *če biz̲uhN̲ni rähpni čuluh rähp lyoon*
   when arrived-he saying-he who-you saying lion

8. *naräni rähp gonga*
   I-he saying ox-that

9. *ši ruhNlu ree*
   what doing-you here

4. Then he went walking, looking for a man.

5. This lion was going along and came to a steer standing in some trees, and he thought that this was a man.

6. Then he sat down, he took one of his claws in his mouth and drew near to him.

7. When he arrived he said, "Who are you?" said the lion.

8. "I am he," said the ox.

9. "What are you doing here?"

4. Y se puso a buscar un hombre.

5. Cuando este león estaba en el camino, se encontró con un toro que estaba entre los palos y pensó que eso era lo que llamaban hombre.

6. Entonces se sentó, puso una de sus uñas en su boca y se acercó al toro.

7. Cuando llegó junto a él, le dijo —¿Quién eres tú?

8. —Yo soy —dijo el toro.

9. —¿Qué haces aquí?

10. *rähpni   ree   kaguzilazä mano   rähpni   sa?ksi*
    saying-he here resting-I   brother saying-he because

    agulälahZ   špašwanä   narä rähpni
    already-abandoned of-owner-my me   saying-he

11. *la et luhdini   laa   nigii rähpni*
    QM not you-not-he name^is man saying-he

12. *et nahrä dini   laa   nigii rähpni*
    not I   not-he name^is man saying-he

13. *šiš   gunlu   nigii rähpni*
    well^why will-be-you man saying-he

14. *narä rlazä   fiä   donnu   la gulii*
    I   wanting-I will-see-I let's^see-we yes will-straight

    bindaan   nigii rähpni
    person-strong man saying-he

15. *utale   mano*
    my^goodness brother

10. He said, "Here I am resting, brother," he said, "because my owner has abandoned me."

11. "Are you not the one who is called man?" he said.

12. "I am not he who is called man," he said.

13. "Well what would you do with a man?" he (steer) said.

14. "I want to see if it is true that a man is very strong," he said.

15. "My goodness no, brother."

10. —Pues, aquí estoy descansando, hermano —dijo— porque me abandonó mi dueño —dijo.

11. —¿Qué, tú no eres lo que llaman hombre? —dijo él.

12. —Yo no soy lo que llaman hombre —le dijo—.

13. ¿Qué vas a hacer con lo que llaman hombre? —le preguntó.

14. —Quiero ver si es cierto que el hombre es tan fuerte como dicen —dijo.

15. —¡Cielos! No, hermano

16. *rähpni   na?k   čačagdoolu   nigii rähpni   et*
    saying-he not   will-gather-big-you man saying-he not

    cosrodi   nahk nigii rähpni   laksi   te   la? nahk nigii
    thing-big-not was man saying-he how-just one part was man

    per nani laa   nigii kosroru   ruhNni dominaar
    but that name^is man   thing-big-more doing-he dominate

    kwantimaaz   luh
    how^much-just-more you

17. *guliilu   et luh dini rähp   lyoon*
    straightened-you not you not-he saying lion

18. *et nahrä dini   rähp   gonmaaž*
    not I   not-he saying ox-steer

19. *asa?are   rähp lyoon*
    already-go-I-here saying lion

20. *sä'tini   bya?nti   gonmaaž*
    going-just-he   remained-just ox-steer

16. He said, "Do not go meeting a man. He is not a big man," he said, "just a small piece is man. But the one called man is very great to dominate, much more than you."

17. "It is true that you are not he?" said the lion.

18. "I am not he," said the steer.

19. "I am going from here," said the lion.

20. The lion left and the steer stayed there.

16. —dijo—. No vayas buscando al hombre. El hombre no es grande. Es chiquito. Pero es bueno para dominar. Mucho más que tú.

17. —Entonces, ¿En verdad tú no eres? —dijo el león.

18. —Yo no soy —dijo el toro.

19. —Ya me voy —dijo el león.

20. Y se fue el león, pero el toro se quedó.

21. *če   bizuhNni   stee   laht   suga? te   mandip*
    when arrived-he another place   stand one animal-healthy

22. *sas rähpni   la   luh ni   laa   nigii rähpni*
    and saying-he QM you that name^is   man saying-he

23. *et   nahrä dini   mano   rähpni*
    not I   not-he brother saying-he

24. *ši   gunlu   nigii rähp mandip*
    what will-be-you man   saying animal-healthy

25. *narä rlazä   fiä   gidonnu   la gulii   ni*
    I   wanting-I will-see-I will-let's^see-we QM will-straight that

    ruzä'treni   nahk ni   laa   nigii rähpni
    talking^about-they was that name^is man saying-he

26. *ryehN dyagä nahreni bindaan   nigii bindanduš*
    hearing ear-I say-they person-strong man person-strong-very

    nigii
    man

21. When he arrived at another place, there was a beast of burden.

22. Then he said, "Are you called man?"

23. "I am not he, brother," he said.

24. "What do you want to do with man?" said the beast of burden.

25. "I want to see if it is true what they say about the one called man," he said.

26. "I have heard that they say a man is very strong, very, very strong."

21. Cuando el león llegó a otro lugar, estaba allí una bestia.

22. El león le dijo a la bestia:
    —¿Eres lo que llaman hombre?

23. —Yo no soy, hermano —dijo él—.

24. ¿Qué quieres con el hombre?

25. —Quiero verlo a ver si es cierto lo que he oído del mentado hombre.

26. Oigo que dicen que el hombre es fuerte, muy fuerte —dijo.

27. *aii mano*
    oh brother

28. *rähpni   na?k čačagdoolu   nigii rähpni   sa?ksi nigii*
    saying-he not will-gather-big-you man saying-he because man

    pwes nigiipakzani   rähpni
    well man-truly-also-he saying-he

29. *pwes laktižini   rähp lyoon*
    well how-just-he-it saying lion

30. *et kwentrodi   nahk nigii rähpni   per nigiini rähpni*
    not story-big-not was man saying-he but man-he saying-he

31. *guliilu   et luhdini   rähpni*
    straightened-you not you-not-him saying-he

32. *et   nahrä dini   rähpni*
    not I   not-he saying-he

33. *asa?are   pwes rähpni*
    already-go-I-here well saying-he

27. "Oh, brother."

28. He said, "Don't you go to meet
    a man, because, well, he is truly
    a man."

29. "How (big) is he?" said the lion.

30. "He is not of great size," he
    said, "but he is a man."

31. "Is it true that you are not he?"
    he said.

32. "I am not he," he said.

33. "Well, I am going from here,"
    he said.

27. —¡Pobre hermano! —dijo—.

28. No vayas a buscar al hombre,
    porque el hombre es muy duro.

29. —¿Pues, qué tanto? —dijo el
    león.

30. —Su estatura no es muy grande
    —dijo—, pero es hombre.

31. —¿Es verdad que tú no eres el
    hombre? —le preguntó.

32. —Yo no soy —le contestó.

33. —Ya me voy —dijo el león.

34. *sä'tini*
   going-just-he

35. *če bizuhNni stee laht suga? te kabaii*
   when arrived-he another place stand one horse

36. *rähpni lohni la luh ni nahk nigii rähpni*
   saying-he to-him QM you that was man saying-he

37. *et nahrä dini rähpni et nahrä di nakä nigii*
   not I   not-he saying-he not I   not almost-be-I man

   rähpni
   saying-he

38. *šiš gunlu nigii rähpni*
   well^why will-be-you man saying-he

39. *rlazä fiä lo nigii gidon lakti nigii*
   wanting-I will-see-I to man will-let's^see how-just man

40. *ryehN dyagä nahreni bendaanni nigii rähpni*
   hearing ear-I say-they person-strong-he man saying-he

34. And he just left.

35. When he arrived at another place, a horse was standing there.

36. He said to him, "Are you a man?"

37. "I am not he," he said "I am not a man."

38. "Well what do you want with a man?" he said.

39. "I want to see a man to see just how big a man is.

40. I have heard them say that a man is very strong," he said.

34. Y se fue.

35. Cuando llegó a otro lugar, se encontró con un caballo.

36. Le preguntó: —¿Eres tú un hombre?

37. —No —dijo—, yo no soy un hombre.

38. ¿Qué vas a hacer con un hombre? —le preguntó.

39. —Quiero ver un hombre para saber qué tan grande es.

40. He oído decir que el hombre es muy fuerte —dijo.

41. *beṇdanduš   nigii rähpni*
   person-strong-very man saying-he

42. *rlazä   gudedä   preeb kon nigii gidonnu   rähpni*
   wanting-I will-pass-I test   with man will-let's^see-we saying-he

   lyoon
   lion

43. *naʔk čawalluni   rähp kabaii saʔksi   narä če*
   not will-touch-you-him saying horse because I   when

   gukä   meer biʔn   Luš rapdušä   fres   rähpni
   made-I almost young^man and had-very-I strength saying-he

   gunaaz te   nigii narä biʔnni
   grabbed one man me   young^man-he

44. *gubihBni narä*
   rode-he me

45. *basaksíni   narä bažuṇnähni narä rähpni*
   punished-he me   ran-with-he me   saying-he

41. "Man is very strong," he (horse) said.

41. —El hombre es muy fuerte —le dijo el caballo.

42. "I want to have a test with the man to see," said the lion.

42. —Quiero hacerle una prueba al hombre para que yo sepa —dijo el león.

43. "Don't you touch him," said the horse, "because when I was young and had lots of strength, a man caught me, a young one."

43. —No lo vayas a tocar —dijo el caballo— porque cuando yo era joven y tenía mucho fuerza —le dijo—, me agarró uno de ellos; uno joven.

44. "He rode me."

44. Y me montó.

45. "He punished me and he ran with me," he said.

45. Me castigó y me hizo correr con él montado sobre mí —dijo.

46. *guyäpsäbä gunibdušaʔ*   *te*   *gitehBni*   *loh* *yuh*   *dini*
    broke-I   moved^about that will-fall-he to   ground not-he

    nitehB   *rähpni*
    almost-fall saying-he

47. *bastooni*   *narä niʔkni*   *rniä*   *naʔk*
    cause-tamed-he I   therefore-that saying-I not

    čačagtooluni   *saʔksi*   *peligros*   *nahk* *ni*   *laa*
    will-gather-tame-you-he because dangerous was   that name^is

    nigii rähpni
    man   saying-he

48. *niluš narä rapä*   *gust rähp*   *lyoon fiä*   *donnu*
    then   I   tending-I like saying lion   will-see-I let's^see-we

    laktičaza   *ni*   *laa*   *nigii rähpni*
    how-just-perhaps-also that name^is man   saying-he

49. *mbah rähpni*   *witiḷḷuni*   *rähpni*
    OK   saying-he go-look-you-him saying-he

46. "I jumped and I moved various ways in order that he would fall to the ground, but he did not fall," he said.

47. "He tamed me, therefore, I am saying to you, do not try to tame him because the one called man is dangerous," he said.

48. "But I have this desire," said the lion, "to see just how great perhaps this one called man is."

49. "OK," he said. "You go look for him," he said.

46. Y por más que brinqué e hice toda clase de movimientos bruscos para que se cayera al suelo —dijo—, no lo logré.

47. Él me amansó —dijo—. Por eso te estoy diciendo que no vayas a jugar con el hombre, porque es muy peligroso.

48. —Pero yo tengo el deseo —dijo el león— de ver el tamaño de eso que llaman hombre.

49. —Bueno —dijo—, ve a buscarlo, pues.

50. *sä'ti   lyoon*
    going-just   lion

51. *zit-ziht sääni*
    far-far   going-he

52. *bizuhNni   yehk te   dahN*
    arrived-he head one mountain

53. *sobga?ni   ro?k   kayuhNni   šigab   donnu   kanehZ*
    sit-lying-he there doing-he   thought let's^see-we where-way

    gisah   ni   laa   nigii laktiza   ni   laa   nigii
    will-appear   that name^is man how-just-also that name^is man

54. *sobga?tini   ro?k*
    sit-lying-just-he there

55. *če   byehN   dyahGni kadin yahG gaše?   dahN*
    when heard   ear-he   cut   tree near-little mountain

50. And the lion was going.

51. Far, far he was going.

52. He arrived at the top of a mountain.

53. He was sitting there thinking, trying to figure out where the man would appear, the one who was powerful.

54. He was just sitting there.

55. When he heard the cutting of wood nearby on the mountain.

50. Y el león se fue.

51. Fue muy lejos.

52. Llegó a la cima de un cerro.

53. Y se sentó allí pensando dónde aparecería el hombre de tamaño tan grande.

54. Sólo estaba sentado allí,

55. cuando oyó que alguien estaba cortando leña en la montaña cercana.

56. *gwen gwen rahk   dahN   kadin yahG roʔk bah*
    gwen gwen making mountain cutting wood there OK

57. *utale   naani mbahY nah siini   decši   laa*
    my^goodness say-he OK   now will-see-he that-he name^is

    nigii naani mbah nah čaʔapak donnu   la gulii
    man say-he OK   now go-I-truly let's^see-we QM will-straight

    bendaan   nigii naani
    person-strong man say-he

58. *sas gulääni loh bišugnaani   sä'tini*
    and took-he to   toenail-hand-his going-just-he

59. *sää sääni   če   gahš asaẓuhNni   byakǰi*
    going going-he when near already-go-arrive-he was-quiet

60. *jehk kayuhNni šigab   naani kanehZgani   naani*
    then doing-he thought say-he where-way-that-he say-he

56. Guen, guen was the noise coming from the mountain where the wood was being cut.

57. "My goodness," he thought, "now I will go and there see he who is called man." "Now I will truly know if it is true that man is very strong," he thought.

58. He took out his toenails and he left.

59. He went and he went, but when he came close, it was quiet.

60. Then he thought, "Where is he anyway?"

56. ¡Tris, tras!, sonaba en la montaña donde se estaba cortando la leña.

57. "¡Órale!", pensó, "ahora sí voy a poder ver al que llaman hombre. Ahora sí voy a ver si es de veras muy grande."

58. Sacó sus uñas y fue.

59. Él caminó y caminó, pero cuando ya estaba cerca, todo estaba en silencio.

60. Entonces pensó otra vez: "¿pero dónde está él?"

61. *jehk guslosak   kadin   yahG stee   niluš garenka   nehZ*
    then began-again cutting wood again then different-also way

    bačaloni   mbah saʔksi   kah   šseʔ   dahN
    thought-he OK   because put of-voice mountain

62. *jehk gunaazni   garenka   nehZ biẓuhNni nehZ kadro*
    then grabbed-he different-also way   arrived-he way   where

    bačalooni   naani   nezreeži
    thought-he say-he way-here-he

63. *niluš byakjisak*
    then was-quiet-again

64. *jehk gurehni kayuhNni šigab   naani kanehZgani   naani*
    then sat-he   doing-he thought say-he where-way-that-he say-he

65. *če   guslosak   yahG kadin nez rekli   kadin yahG*
    when began-again wood cutting way there-much cutting tree

    Luš laani nez rekli   yuʔni
    and he   way there-much is-he

61. Then it began again, cutting another tree in another place he thought, because of what the mountain did to the sound.

62. Then the lion took another trail. When he arrived where he thought the man was, he said, "He is this way."

63. But it was quiet again.

64. Then he sat down and he was thinking, "What way is he?"

65. When a tree was being cut again, it was this way (direction) that it was being cut, and it was this way that he was.

61. Cuando el hombre empezó a cortar otro árbol, el sonido venía de otro lugar debido a la forma en que la montaña afectaba al sonido.

62. Entonces tomó otro camino pensando que de allí venía el ruido. Cuando llegó al lugar pensó: "Aquí es".

63. Pero el sonido cesó y se hizo el silencio otra vez.

64. Entonces se sentó y se puso a pensar: "¿Pero, dónde es?"

65. Cuando empezaron a cortar otro árbol, el ruido venía de cerca de donde él estaba.

66. *ǰehkti   batyuugni nehZ naani ǰehk nez reeži   naani*
    then-just cut-he   way say-he then way here-he say-he

    gunaaztini   nehZ sääni
    grabbed-just-he way   going-he

67. *sä'tini*
    going-just-he

68. *ǰehk če   biʒuhNni lo nigii rähp lyoon la luhni*
    then when arrived-he to man saying lion QM you-he

69. *naräni rähpni   la yu? ši   rlahZlu   rähpni*
    I-he   saying-he QM is what wanting-you saying-he

70. *la luh ni laa   nigii rähpni*
    QM you that name^is   man   saying-he

71. *naräni rähpni   ši   gunlu   narä rähpni*
    I-he   saying-he what will-be-you I   saying-he

66. Then he cut the path, he thought this way (direction) he is, and he took this path and he went.

67. He was just going.

68. When he arrived to the man the lion said, "Are you he?"

69. "I am he," said the man. "What is it that you want?"

70. "Are you (he) who is called man?" he said.

71. "I am he," he said. "What do you want with me?"

66. Entonces cortó su camino y dijo: "Por aquí es". Y siguió otro camino.

67. Siguió caminando.

68. Cuando llegó a donde estaba el hombre le preguntó: —¿Eres tú?

69. —Yo soy —dijo—. ¿Qué quieres?

70. —¿Eres tú lo que llaman hombre? —le preguntó

71. —Yo soy —dijo—. ¿Qué quieres conmigo?

72. *rapä   gust   gikwaanu   teh   rähp   lyoon*
    having-I like   will-nail-we one   saying lion

73. *na?k mano   rähpni   sa?ksi   luh   mandušlu   rähpni*
    not   brother saying-he because you   animal-very-you saying-he

74. *sobga?tini*
    sit-lying-just-he

75. *Rähp lyoon gikwaanu   rähpni   rapäpak   gust gikwaanu*
    saying lion   will-nail-we saying-he   having-I-truly like will-nail-we

    teh gidonnu   la   gulii   bendaanlu   rähpni
    one   will-let's^see-we QM   straight person-strong-you saying-he

76. *mbah rähpni   gulahZ   gutyazä   yahG   štenä   rähpni   te*
    OK   saying-he will-wait   will-split-I wood   of-my   saying-he that

    jehktiru   gikwaanu   rähpni
    then-just-more   will-nail-we saying-he

77. *mbah rähp   lyoon*
    OK   saying lion

72. "I want that we would fight,"
    said the lion.

73. "No brother," he said. "You are
    a big animal.

74. He was just sitting there.

75. The lion said, "Let's fight. I truly
    must fight you to see if you are
    strong."

76. "OK," he said. "Wait until I
    finish splitting my wood, then we
    will fight."

77. "OK," said the lion.

72. —Quiero que peleemos —dijo el
    león.

73. —No, hermano —le contestó el
    hombre—, porque tú eres un ani-
    mal grande.

74. Él estaba nada más allá sentado.

75. —Vamos a pelear —le decía el
    león—. Tengo que pelear conti-
    go para saber si de veras eres
    muy fuerte.

76. —Bueno —le dijo—, espérate
    que raje mi palo, y luego pelea-
    mos.

77. —Bueno —dijo el león.

78. *basahBni te gibyahG bigas škibyahGni lajd kort*
    put-he one iron-tree stuck of-iron-tree-his place cut

79. *nah žo gunni mbah nasni gibyahG*
    now how will-be-he OK stuck-he iron-tree

    kagusniibnini dizani gun gaan kwääniži
    cause-moving-he-it not-also-it will-be gain take^out-he-it

80. *koorlu sobga? sobga?tis lyoon*
    what-hour-you sit-lying sit-lying-only lion

81. *mbah rähp nigii palga yu?paklu gaan gikwaanu gudaa*
    OK saying man if-that is-truly-you gain will-nail-we come

    gaknählu gibäänu škibyagä ree rähpni
    will-be-with-you will-take-we of-iron-wood-my here saying-he

82. *yo rähp lyoon*
    OK saying lion

83. *gubig lyoon*
    drew^near lion

78. He put in his ax and it got stuck in the cut.

79. What would he do now! His ax was stuck and his moving it did not unstick it.

80. Until what hour sat that lion!

81. "OK," said the man, "if you really want to fight, come, you will help with my ax. We will take it from this cut."

82. "Yes," said the lion.

83. The lion drew near.

78. Al bajar el hacha, se le quedó atorada en el árbol.

79. ¡Qué iba a hacer ahora? Su hacha estaba atorada, y por mucho que la movía no lograba sacarla.

80. Y el león seguía allí sentado.

81. —Bueno —le dijo el hombre—, si de veras quieres pelear, ven a ayudarme a sacar mi hacha.

82. —Sí —dijo el león.

83. El león se acercó.

84. *guslohni kabääni gibyahG baki?¢ naani   lajd   kort mbah*
    began-he taking-he iron-tree rubbed hand-his place cut OK

85. *niluš dini   gun   gaan te   laad saa wihni   baki?¢ni*
    then not-he will-be gain one place then went-he rubbed-he

    girop laad naani   bašalni   yahGga
    two   side hand-his opened-he wood-that

86. *če   guläs nigii gibyahG pwes bijya?n   naani   lajd*
    when took man   iron-tree well going-remain hand-his place

    cortga bijya?n   patnaaži   ro?k
    cut-that going-remain paw-hand-his there

87. *mbah nah siini   rähp nigii gikwaanu nah rähpni*
    OK   now going-it saying man will-nail-we now saying-he

88. *jehkti   gunaazni   lyoon tehš*
    then-just grabbed-he lion   one

89. *kon garo?t bawahkWni lyoon*
    with whip whipped-he lion

84. He began to take out the ax, he was rubbing his paw in the cut place.

85. He did not get it on one side, so he went on both sides with his paws to open up that wood.

86. When the man took out the ax, well his (lion) paws remained in the cut. His paws were stuck there!

87. "OK, now it will be," said the man. "Now we will fight."

88. Then he grabbed the lion.

89. With the whip he beat the lion.

84. Él empezó a sacar el hacha. Metió las patas en la ranura del tronco.

85. Pero no las metió sólo de un lado, sino que en los dos lados de la madera.

86. Cuando aquel hombre sacó el hacha, las patas del león se quedaron en la ranura. ¡Estaban trabadas!

87. —Bueno, ahora sí —dijo el hombre—, vamos a pelear.

88. Entonces el hombre agarró al león.

89. Con un látigo golpeó al león.

90. *behN perdon narä rähp   lyoon*
    made pardon me   saying lion

91. *pwes šeti perdon rähp   nigii saʔksi   rlahZlu   kwanählu*
    well not pardon saying man   because wanting-you nail-with-you

    narä
    me

92. *skreeza   nakä   narä rähpni*
    way-also is-be-I I   saying-he

93. *ĵehk guslonähni   lyoon tehš gunabli   lyoon perdon*
    then began-with-he lion   one asked-much lion   pardon

    rähpni   behN perdon amigW rähpni   amigw jyaʔcnu
    saying-he made pardon friend saying-it friend will-make-we

94. *naʔk juʔtlu   narä*
    not will-kill-you me

95. *naʔk juʔtlu   narä rähpni   te   jyaʔcnu   amigW*
    not will-kill-you me   saying-he that will-make-we friend

90. "Forgive me," said the lion.

91. "But there is no forgiveness," said the man, "because you wanted to fight me."

92. "This is the way it is with me," said the man.

93. Then he began to do one on the lion who was just asking forgiveness. He said, "Make forgiveness, friend. We will make it (things right)."

94. "Do not kill me.

95. Do not kill me," said the lion, "in order that we can be friends."

90. —Perdóname —le dijo el león.

91. —Pues no hay perdón —dijo el hombre—, porque tú querías pelear conmigo.

92. Así son las cosas conmigo —dijo.

93. Pues comenzó a golpear al león. Y el león pedía perdón.

94. —No me mates.

95. No me mates —dijo el león— para que podamos hacernos amigos.

96. *šetidi   rähp   nigii saʔksi   palga narä guslaalu*
    not-just-not saying man because if-that I   will-cause-free-you

    sahWlu   narä
    will-eat-you me

97. *dina gawälu*
    not-I will-eat-I-you

98. *behN perdon narä rähpni*
    made pardon me   saying-he

99. *atanto pwes behN nigii perdonži*
    much   well made man   pardon-him

100. *jehk baslaa   nigiiži*
     then caused-free man-him

101. *če   baslaa   nigiiži jehkti   behNreni desperdiir*
     when caused-free man-him then-just made-they good^bye

     saʔreži rähpži   bainah siini   jyaknu   amigW
     kind-them saying-he OK-now going-he will-is-we friend

     rähpni
     saying-he

96. "No," said the man. "If I free you, you will eat me."

97. "I will not eat you.

98. Forgive me," he said.

99. At last that man forgave him.

100. Then the man freed him.

101. When the man freed the lion, they said their goodbyes and the lion said, "OK now we will be friends."

96. —No —dijo el hombre—, si te suelto, tú me vas a comer.

97. —No te comeré.

98. Perdóname —dijo.

99. Y de tanto que le pidió, el hombre lo perdonó.

100. Entonces lo soltó.

101. Cuando el hombre soltó al león, entonces se despidieron, y el león dijo: —Vamos a ser amigos.

102. *reʔtinah   palga   gun   tokaar tedlu   karo   yuʔä*
     gather-just-now if-that will-be touch   pass-you where is-I

   rähpni   narä gudedloälu   te   di   saklu   kasyoon
   saying-he I   will-pass-to-I-you that not will-be-you danger

103. *jyaʔcnu   amigW   mano   rähpni*
     will-make-we friend brother saying-he

104. *basadiijti   saʔreni*
     make-set-word-just kind-their

105. *gunii roʔk behN despedeer saʔni   bireʔčtireni*
     said there made farewell   kind-it scattered-just-they

   sä'tireni
   going-just-they

106. *roʔkti   syäläti   jehk   komp*
     there-just going-I-just   then   friend

107. *guluhštiži*
     finished-just-it

102. "From now on," he said, "if I meet you, I will pass by you so that there will not be danger.

103. We will be friends now, brother," he said.

104. And they made firm their word together.

105. They said their goodbyes and they separated. They were just going.

106. There I left then, friend.

107. It is finished.

102. De aquí en adelante si estoy por donde tú estás, yo pasaré de largo para que no haya peligro.

103. Seremos amigos, hermano —dijo.

104. Y se despidieron.

105. Allí se despidieron y se separaron. Se fue cada uno por su lado.

106. Allí, no más, yo también me fui.

107. Y el cuento se terminó.

The Man Who Went to Town

Manuel Quero Olivero

1. *yuʔ te behN̲ wihni te gehǰ*
   is   one person went-he one town

2. *wisiini   ši   rekos ni   rkiinni*
   bought-he what things that being-necessary-he

3. *nahkni te behN̲ ni   yuʔ lo renč*
   was-it one person that is   on ranch

1. There was a man who went to town.	1. Había una vez un hombre que fue al pueblo.
2. He went to buy the things that he needed.	2. Fue al pueblo a comprar sus provisiones.
3. He was a person from the ranch.	3. Él vivía en el rancho.

4. *če   biriini   lo tyendga agusiini   giraa ši*
   when came^out-he to store-that already-bought-he all what

   kos   štenni
   thing of-him

5. *jehk syädnäni   te mul kon te bä'kW*
   then coming-with-he one mule where one dog

6. *jehkni   basguuni   mul rek   kargw rešikos   ni*
   then-that caused-loaded-he mule there cargo what-things that

   gusiini   basguunini
   bought-he caused-loaded-he-it

7. *per ya če abii   mulreni jehk nadti   mulre*
   but yes when already-loaded mule-they then not-just mule-this

   sa
   walk

8. *alga   rbeh   mul*
   better sitting mule

4. When he came out of the store, he had purchased all that he needed.

4. Después que compró todas sus mercancías, salió de la tienda.

5. He came with his mule and his dog.

5. Había venido con su mula y su perro.

6. Then he loaded his mule with the things he had bought.

6. Entonces cargó todas las cosas que había comprado en la mula.

7. But when he loaded the things on the mule, the mule decided not to walk.

7. Pero cuando la mula se sintió cargada, no quiso caminar.

8. Better for the mule to sit.

8. Y decidió que era mejor echarse.

9. *jehk kwaʔni   te   garoʔt*
   then will-take-he one whip

10. *guslohni kawahkWni mul kagihNni mul*
    began-he whipping-he mule hitting-he mule

11. *jehk al   maazru   raa   mul*
    then already more-more shrivel mule

12. *guslohni   kageni   lo mul basqehNga*
    will-begin-he swearing-he to mule caused-hurried-up-that

    wistye   te doʔä rähpni
    caused-stood that go-I saying-he

13. *jehk tant ni kagihNni mul bawiini katehB nis   lo mul*
    then much that hitting-he mule saw-he fall   water eye mule

14. *jehk rwii   rwiitis   mul loni*
    then seeing seeing-manner mule on-him

15. *jehkni   čela   guniila mul*
    then-that when-yes said-yes mule

9. Then the man took a whip.

10. Then he started whipping the mule and hitting the mule.

11. Then the mule shrank back more.

12. Then he started swearing at the mule: "Hurry up there, stand up in order that I can go," he said.

13. Very much he was hitting that mule, and tears began to fall from the mule's eyes.

14. And the mule looked, he was looking very sad to him.

15. And then that mule spoke.

9. El hombre cogió entonces un garrote.

10. Y empezó a golpear a la mula y a insultarla.

11. Pero la mula permanecía echada.

12. Entonces el hombre empezó a insultar a la mula: —¡Apúrate, lavántate y vámonos! —le decía.

13. Le pegó tanto, que la mula empezó a llorar.

14. Y se le quedó mirando tristemente.

15. Y de repente la mula habló.

16. *rähpni   naʔkru   rgihNlu   narä rähpni*
    saying-he not-more hitting-you me   saying-he

17. *jehk bijebdušni   byehN dyahGni*
    then afraid-very-he made   ear-he

18. *weno byehN dyahGni gunii mulre*
    OK   made ear-he   said mule-this

19. *ružundušni   biriini   ružunni   sääni*
    running-very-he came^out-he running-he going-he

20. *nikla   laani dini gan   kanehZ   ginyaazni*
    neither he   not-he will-know where-way will-grab-he

    sažuntisni   sažuntisni   lo te nezyuh
    go-run-manner-he go-run-manner-he on one way-ground

21. *jehktini   hasta kadro abajagliini   sažunni*
    then-just-that until where already-tired-straight-he go-run-he

    hasta luhjni   akabääni
    until tongue-his already-taking-he

16. He said, "Don't you hit me any more."

17. Then the man was very afraid when he heard this mule talking.

18. He heard this mule speak!

19. He was running very hard, he left, he ran as he was leaving.

20. He did not know what way he should run; he just ran, he ran down a trail.

21. Then he ran to where he was completely tired out, until his tongue was hanging out.

16. Le dijo al hombre: —Ya no me pegues más.

17. El hombre recibió un gran susto al oír hablar a la mula.

18. ¡Había oído hablar a la mula!

19. Y salió corriendo de aquel lugar.

20. No sabía ni qué dirección seguir, sólo corría y corría.

21. Iba ya con la lengua de fuera. Corrió y corrió hasta que cayó agotado.

22. *sarinaļgahk*   *špä'kWnini sigahkza špä'kWni*
    go-go-follow-immediately of-dog-his-it like-also of-dog-his

    abajahGni
    already-tired-he

23. *gurehni kazilahZni teraʔt*
    sat-he   resting-he little

24. *jehk näh špä'kWni gureh nez lohni*
    then with of-dog-he sat   way to-him

25. *jehk čela   gunii špä'kWni rähp   špä'kWni lohni   lakti*
    then when-yes said   of-dog-he saying of-dog-his to-him how-just

    bațehB mul nurnu oʔ
    scared mule us   yes

22. His dog was following him too, and in like manner his dog was tired.

23. The man sat down to rest a little.

24. Then his dog sat down facing him.

25. His dog sitting in front of him said, "How very much that mule scared us, didn't he."

22. El perro también corrió asustado detrás de su amo, y también estaba agotado.

23. El hombre se sentó a descansar un rato.

24. Y su perro se sentó enfrente de él.

25. Entonces el perro, que estaba sentado frente a él, habló y le dijo —¡Qué susto nos dio la mula!, ¿verdad?

A Person of the Earth Who Was Cold All the Time

Manuel Quero Olivero

1. *yuʔ te ben gejlyuh nani entis raknahLni yuʔni*
   is one person town-earth that just^only being-cold-he is-he

   lo gejlyuhre
   on town-earth-this

2. *jehk če guhtni wihni gibaa*
   then when died-he went-he sky

1. There was a person of this earth that was just cold all the time.

2. When he died he went to heaven.

1. Había una persona en este mundo que todo el tiempo tenía frío.

2. Cuando murió, se fue al cielo.

3. *sigahkza yuʔni roʔk entis   raknahLni   če   bawii San*
   like-also is-he there just^only being-cold-he when saw   San

   Pedr entis   rakdihtni   jiuʔni   gibaa
   Pedro just^only being-shaking-he will-enter-he sky

4. *jehkti   ginii   behN San   Pedr   šigab   narä mejor*
   then-just will-say made Saint Peter thought I   better

   gušaläni   gak   ster't   roʔk nanlaa te   kuesčaʔ
   will-sent-I-him will-be little^time there hot   that will-warm

   škwerpni
   of-body-his

5. *jehk guninäni   benjab rähpni   lo benjab guräh gunijä*
   then said-with-he devil   saying-he to devil   polite will-give-I

   behN   redohLlu guzälaaluni   nen te   yuʔ   kadro
   person sins-your will-hold-favor-you-him in   one house where

   najaʔ   kadro yuʔrureni   te   kuesčaʔni
   is-warm where is-more-them in^order^that will-warm-he

---

3. He was also cold when Saint
   Peter saw him, he was shaking
   as he entered heaven.

4. Just then Saint Peter thought,
   "It's better I should send him to
   be a little while over there
   where it is hot in order that he
   can warm his body."

5. Then he spoke to the devil, he
   said to him, "I will give a person
   with sins to you. You put him in
   a room where it is warm, where
   there are more (in order) that
   he be warmed.

3. Cuando lo vio San Pedro, temblando nada más, al entrar al
   cielo,

4. se dijo: "¡Qué barbaridad! mejor
   lo mando por un rato a donde
   está caliente, para que se caliente su cuerpo".

5. Entonces, habló con el diablo, y
   le dijo con mucha cortesía: —Le
   voy a dar a una persona con pe-
   cados para que ponga en un
   cuarto donde haya más gente para calentarla.

6. *mbah rähp ste   benjab*
   OK   saying more person-evil

7. *basäḻ benjab   neṉ primeer yuʔä*
   put person-evil in first   house-my

8. *roʔk naa benjabni gaiitis   minut guzäläni   tianti jehk*
   there say devil-he five-only minute will-place-I-him just then

   jiaʔnni   ṉah
   will-leave-he now

9. *basäḻreni roʔk gaii minut*
   put-they there five minute

10. *če   guhk behṈ biäḻlahZ   te   yuʔ ¢uu minut roʔk*
    when was person remembered one is ten minute there

    gužuṉni wijaag gužuṉni te   ši bawiini
    will-run-he met   will-run-he inˆorderˆthat what saw-he

    laḻti   rakdiht   behṈga
    while-just being-shaking person-that

6. "OK" said the other demon.

6. —Bueno —dijo el demonio.

7. Then the demon sent (him) to his first house.

7. Entonces el demonio lo mandó a su primer cuarto.

8. That devil said he would leave him there just five minutes, then he left there.

8. Y le dijo: —Solamente vas a estar aquí cinco minutos —y lo dejó.

9. They put (him) there for five minutes.

9. Lo puso allí por cinco minutos.

10. When that person remembered, it was ten minutes there, he ran in order to see (that person). Well that person was just shaking.

10. Cuando esa persona se dio cuenta, ya habían pasado diez minutos. El diablo corrió y vio que esta persona seguía temblando.

11. *jehk naani nani gujvälnuni   ni   riohNli   kuartgani*
    then say-he that will-find-we-he that third-much room-that-it

    ni?k   maazru   najva? nanlaa te   nenga te   nenga
    therefore more-more is-hot hot   that in-that one in-that

    gučaglahZni
    will-gather-heart-he

12. *jehkni   guläänini   ro?k wisälnini   li   ryohN*
    then-that will-take-he-him there put-he-him straight third

    kuartga   ni   maazru   nanlaa
    room-that that more-more hot

13. *bizälni   nani ree čontis   minut čää   behNru*
    threw-he that here three-only minute will-go person-more

    ree porque nanladuš nani ši   gakni
    here because hot-very that what will-be-it

14. *jehk šikwent gudedä   loh San Pedr benjab   šigabni*
    then why   will-pass-I to Saint Peter person-evil thought-his

11. Then he said that we would find
    him a third room, one that is
    hotter, one that his heart would
    enjoy.

11. Entonces dijo que le iba a bus-
    car un cuarto más caliente; un
    cuarto tan caliente que le iba a
    encantar.

12. He was put there for only three
    minutes more because it would
    be really hot.

12. Lo puso allí por tres minutos so-
    lamente, porque iba a estar de
    veras caliente.

13. He was thrown there for only
    three minutes; this person
    (would go) there because it
    would be really hot.

13. Lo puso allí por tres minutos
    porque allí estaría mucho más
    caliente.

14. "Then what will I give to Saint
    Peter," that demon thought.

14. "Luego si le pasa algo", pensaba
    el diablo, "¿qué le voy a decir a
    San Pedro?".

15. *ȷ̌ehkru   če   gohL   čoṉ   minut   če   wišalni   roʔk*
    then-more when happened three minute when opened-he there

   la   kayacnahḺ   behṈ   reʔk   yuʔ
   QM being-cold   person there   house

16. *gunaani pwes mejor gisäḻnuni   ni   rahk   gaii   kuartga*
    said-he well better will-put-we-he that make   five   room-that

   neṉga   sii   naṉladuš ganaž   lo   bahḺ   yuʔni   neṉga   fii
   in-that yes hot-very first on   fire   is-it   in-that seeing

   fiinu   la   donnu   žo   rčalo   behṈre
   seeing-we QM let's^see-we how think person-this

17. *gunaazreni   basäḻrenini   kadro naṉladuš roʔk*
    grabbed-they put-they-him   where hot-very there

18. *ȷ̌ehk nahni teh minut čääni basäureni roʔk*
    then say-he one minute go-he closed-they there

19. *ȷ̌ehk kagihtreni*
    then playing-they

15. Then when three minutes had
    passed, he went to open there;
    was that person cold there in
    the room?

15. Cuando pasaron tres minutos,
    fue a abrir (la puerta). ¿Tendría
    frío la persona en ese cuarto?

16. He said, "Well it is better that
    we put him in the fifth room. In
    there, yes it is very hot, just on
    fire that room. We'll see, we will
    know how this person likes it!"

16. Entonces la pondremos en el
    quinto cuarto; es más caliente
    allí adentro, porque hay lumbre.
    Vamos a ver qué le parece a es-
    ta persona.

17. Well they grabbed him and put
    him where it was very hot.

17. Pues la agarraron y la pusieron
    donde estaba muy caliente.

18. Then he said one minute he
    would go. They closed it there.

18. Luego dijo que la iba a ponerla
    allí sólo un minuto. La encerra-
    ron allí.

19. Then they were playing.

19. Luego se pusieron a jugar.

20. *biällahZreni   yuʔ behN   rek   nen kuartga*
    remembered-they is   person there in   room-that

21. *če   gukbeereni   aguhkni   te   kuart or   ružunreni*
    when was-remained-they already-was-it one room hour run-they

    wišalreni   roʔ   cuartga   če   bawiireni abehN   yuʔ
    opened-they mouth room-that when saw-they already-person is

    hasta nez rek jehk rähp behNga   kon   säuu   roʔ
    until way there then saying person-this where will-close mouth

    puertga   porque lakti   bennahL   yuʔreni nen ree
    door-that because how-just person-cold is-they in here

    rähpni
    saying-he

22. *žroʔkru   žroʔkru   yuʔni*
    of-there-more of-there-more is-it

20. They remembered there was a person there in that room.

21. When they knew (remembered), fifteen minutes had passed. They ran, they opened that door to the room and when they looked in, that person was there; then he said, "Well close the door to the room because how very cold the people are who are here in this room!"

22. How could there be more of it.

20. De repente, recordaron que había una persona en ese cuarto.

21. Y cuando se dieron cuenta, ya habían pasado quince minutos. Corrieron y abrieron la puerta. Cuando vieron a esa persona, les dijo: —¡Cierren esa puerta, porque la gente que está aquí tiene mucho frío!

22. ¡Cómo podría hacer más frío!

The Turtle and the Buzzard

Fausto Sosa

1. *guyu te wält žo laani guyu? te lugaar sas yu?*
   was one time how him was one place and is

   naksilduš   lugaarga
   is-be-much-very place-that

2. *jehkti   yu? te   legw lohza lo nisga*
   then-just is   one turtle to-also to water-that

3. *te wält gubihz nis   lo yuhga   kadro tre?   nis*
   one time dried water on ground-that where gather water

1. There was a time, was one place that there was very much (water) there.	1. Había una vez un lugar donde había mucha agua.
2. There was also a turtle there in that water.	2. También había una tortuga en el agua.
3. One time the water dried up there on the ground.	3. En una ocasión se secó el agua que había sobre la tierra.

135

4. *jehkti   bya?n   legw   sin   nis*
   then-just remained turtle no   water

5. *agubihẓni   šeti nis   naga?   legw   kayohL   legw*
   already-dried-it not water is-lying turtle thirsting turtle

6. *če   gudehD te   golbeȼ   ro?k   jehk   rähp   golbeȼ   ši*
   when passed one buzzard there then saying buzzard what

   kayuhNlu   ree
   doing-you here

7. *naga?si   rähpni   gubihẓ nis   ree   šetruni   nis   ree*
   is-lying-just saying-he dried water here not-more-it water here

8. *ṇah   kayoläni*
   now thirsting-I-it

9. *ṇah   sauälu   rähp   golbeȼ   porque ši   gauä*
   now will-eat-I-you saying buzzard because what will-eat-I

   kagilä   ree
   finding-I here

4. Then the turtle was there with no water.

5. When there was no water left there, the turtle was thirsty.

6. A buzzard passed by there and said to him, "What are you doing here?"

7. "Just lying (here)," he said, "the water is dried up, there is no water here.

8. Now I am thirsty."

9. "Now I will eat you," said the buzzard, "because I will eat what I will find here."

4. Entonces la tortuga no tenía agua.

5. Como no había agua allí, la tortuga tenía sed.

6. Entonces pasó una zopilote y le dijo: —¿Que haces allí?

7. —Sólo estás allí, acostada —dijo—. Ya no hay agua; no hay más agua aquí.

8. No, y ahora yo tengo sed.

9. —Pues yo te voy a comer —dijo el zopilote—, porque yo como lo que encuentro aquí.

10. *Di   rähp   legw   naʔk   gaulu   narä*
    not saying turtle not   will-eat-you   me

11. *mejor   winä   narä   roʔk   te   nis   ree*
    better went-with me   there one   water here

12. *yä'   čeʔn   nis   ree   rähpni   te   gaǰ   xpälä*
    drink some   water here saying-he one   will-wet of-meat-my

    čeʔn   rähpni   porque   palga   gaulu   narä   nah   rähpni
    some   saying-he because if-that will-eat-you   I   now   saying-he

    čagas   xpälä   yehN ree   saʔksi   nabihẓ nabihẓ
    will-stuck of-meat-my neck here because   is-dry is-dry

    xpälä   štenä   rähpni   di   gakdi   gauluni
    of-meat-my of-me   saying-he not   will-be-not   will-eat-you-it

13. *mejor   winäh   narä   roʔk   nis*
    better go-with me   there water

14. *yä'   čeʔn   nis   rähpni*
    drink some   water saying-he

10. "No," said the turtle, "no, you will not eat me.

11. Better that you take me to that water there.

12. I drink a bit of water here," he said "in order to wet my meat." "If you eat me now," he said, "my meat will stick in your neck because my meat is so very dry. "You will not be able to eat it.

13. It is better (you) go with me to that water,

14. (in order to) drink some water." he (turtle) said.

10. —No —dijo la tortuga—, no me comas.

11. Mejor me llevas al agua que está allá.

12. Tomaré un poquito de agua —dijo— para mojar mi carne un poco. Si me comes ahora, mi carne se va a atorar en tu garganta. Porque ahorita está muy seca mi carne —dijo—; no podrás comerme así.

13. Es mejor que me lleves al agua,

14. para que tome un poco de agua —le dijo la tortuga al zopilote.

15. *la   gulii   rähp   golbeȼ*
    QM straight saying buzzard

16. *guliä   rähp   legw*
    straight-I saying turtle

17. *mbah pwes rähpni   kuah deȼä   rähpni*
    OK   well saying-he put   back-my saying-he

18. *Yoó rähp*
    OK saying

19. *sas kuah legw dehȩni*
    and put   turtle back-his

20. *wä'p golbeȼ jiaro   wä'p golbeȼ*
    went buzzard high-much went buzzard

21. *jehkti   guyuži? legw rlianigw   yehkni*
    then-just was-nose turtle stinking-awful head-his

15. "Is this true?" asked the buzzard.

16. "I am telling the truth," said the turtle.

17. "OK," he (buzzard) said, "get on my back."

18. "OK," he said.

19. Then the turtle got on his back.

20. Up went the buzzard, high went the buzzard.

21. Then the turtle smelled the awful head of the buzzard.

15. —¿Es verdad? —preguntó el zopilote.

16. —Te estoy diciendo la verdad —dijo la tortuga.

17. —Bueno —dijo el zopilote—, súbete a mi espalda.

18. —Bueno —dijo la tortuga.

19. Entonces la tortuga se subió a la espalda del zopilote.

20. Y el zopilote se fue para arriba. Voló muy alto.

21. Entonces la tortuga sintió lo feo que olía la cabeza del zopilote.

22. *jehk   rähp   legw   rähpni   arniä   dadgool*
    then saying turtle saying-he already-saying-I father-old

    rähpni   šikwent rlianigw   yehklu
    saying-he why   stinking-awful head-your

23. *jehkti   ä   rähp   golbeȼ   šikwent rlianehš   yehklu*
    then-just QM saying buzzard why   stinking-sweet head-you

    rähpni
    saying-he

24. *oʔn rähp   golbeȼ   rlianehšni*
    yes saying buzzard stinking-sweet-it

25. *sanänini*
    go-with-he-him

26. *če   biȥuhN golbeȼ   roʔ   nis   sas   rähpni*
    when arrived buzzard mouth water and saying-he

    arniälu   dadgol   rähpni
    already-saying-I-you father-old saying-he

22. Then the turtle said, "I'm saying to you mister, why is your head stinking awful?"

22. Y le dijo: —¿Por qué huele tan feo tu cabeza?

23. Then "What?" the buzzard said, "why does your head smell sweet?"

23. —¿Qué?—dijo el zopilote. —¿Por qué tu cabeza huele dulce?

24. "Yes," said the buzzard, "it smells sweet."

24. —Sí —dijo el zopilote —huele dulce.

25. He went on with him.

25. Y siguió con ella.

26. When the buzzard arrived at the edge of the water, he (turtle) said, "I'm saying (talking) to you mister," he said.

26. Cuando el zopilote llegó cerca del agua, dijo (la tortuga): —Decía a usted señor.

27. *umh rähp   dadgol   la gulii   guht žmamlu*
    yes saying father-mister QM straight died of-grandmother-your

    rähpni
    saying-he

28. *ohNti rähp   dadgol   žo guvxcähBni*
    no-just saying father-mister how will-cause-say-he

    guslaani   ni? legw
    will-cause-free-he foot turtle

29. *nazu?ǫni ni? legw didi   gužun   legw jii   lo nis*
    is-firm-it foot turtle not-not will-run turtle will-go to water

30. *la gulii   guht čäällu   dadgol   rähpni*
    QM straight died spouse-your father-old saying-he

31. *ä rähp   dadgol*
    QM saying father-mister

27. "Yes," said the mister (buzzard). "Is it true your grandmother died?" said the turtle.

27. —Sí —dijo el zopilote. —Murió su abuela, ¿no?—dijo la tortuga.

28. "No," said the mister (buzzard). No way would the buzzard willingly let the turtle's foot to be freed.

28. —No —dijo el zopilote. No quería soltar el pie de la tortuga.

29. The leg of the turtle is firm. Firm the turtle would not run, and enter the water.

29. Tenía agarrado firmemente el pie de la tortuga. Porque sabía que de no tenerla agarrada fuerte, la tortuga correría para meterse al agua.

30. "Is it true your wife died mister (buzzard)?" he (turtle) said.

30. —¿Es verdad que murió su esposa, señor (zopilote)? —dijo la (tortuga).

31. "What?" said the mister (buzzard).

31. —¿Qué? —dijo el señor (zopilote).

32. *čigahsi   gutiähs legw guyuʔ nis*
    then-quietly-just fell   turtle was   water

33. *suhti   golbeȼ*
    sitting-just buzzard

34. *dini   nyahW   legw*
    not-he almost-eat turtle

35. *jehk biʒunnäh   legw lo nis*
    then arrived-with turtle to water

36. *niʔktis   guluhXni*
    this-only finished-it

32. Just quietly the turtle fell into the water.

33. Then the buzzard was just sitting there (alone).

34. He did not eat the turtle.

35. Then the turtle arrived at the water.

36. Just this way it finished.

32. Silenciosamente, la tortuga se metió al agua.

33. El zopilote se quedó allá, sentado solo.

34. No se comió a la tortuga.

35. La tortuga llegó al agua.

36. Y eso es todo.

The Smallest Animal

Manuel Quero Olivero

1. *te   mastr   ni   kaguluii rebyuuž kanabdiiǰni   te   wält   loh*
   one teacher that teaching children asking-word-he one times to

   režpiuužni   rähpni   ču   tehtu   rumbee   čuni?k
   of-children-his saying-he who one-you knowing-straight who

   nahk te   mane?   manbäzru   loh gejlyuhre
   was one animal-little animal-little-more to town-earth-this

2. *ǰehk giraa rebyuuž gureǰi rut rniidi*
   then all   children quiet not saying-not

---

1. A teacher was teaching children. One time he asked them and said, "Who of you knows what the smallest animal of this world is?"

2. Then all the children became quiet, no one said anything.

1. Había un maestro que estaba enseñando a los niños. Un día les preguntó: —¿Cuál es el animal más chico del mundo?

2. Entonces todos los niños se quedaron callados, ninguno hablaba.

143

3. *ǰehk wisu te biužbäzeʔ   rähpni   narä mastr   narä*
   then stood one child-little-little saying-he I   teacher me

   rähpni   narä nanä   čuniʔk
   saying-he I   know-I who

4. *gunii   don   rähp   mastr*
   youˆsay let'sˆsee saying teacher

5. *ǰehk rähpni   maneʔga   laa   čeriskuis rähpni*
   then saying-he animal-little-that nameˆis cheriscuis saying-he

6. *ah rähp   mastr   ču   maneʔga*
   ah saying teacher who animal-little-that

7. *dina gumbeäni   rähpni*
   not-I will-know-I-it saying-he

8. *laaga manbäzeʔ   ni   yuʔ yehk rebeʔȼ räpgahk*
   is-that animal-little-little that is   head fleas   saying-immediately

   biužeʔga
   child-little-that

3. "I do, teacher," he said, "I know what it is."

3. —Yo maestro—dijo un niño—; yo sé la respuesta.

4. "Say it, let's see," said the teacher.

4. —Dila, a ver—dijo el maestro.

5. Then he said, "The name of that little animal is cheriscuis."

5. Entonces el niño dijo: —Es el animal que se llama cheriscuis —dijo.

6. "Oh," said the teacher, "what is this animal?

6. —¡Ah! —dijo el maestro—, ¿y qué animal es ése?

7. I do not know it," he said.

7. Yo no lo conozco —dijo.

8. "It is the animal that lives on the head of a flea," said that child.

8. —Es un animal chico que vive en la cabeza de una pulga —dijo el niño.

CPSIA information can be obtained
at www.ICGtesting.com
Printed in the USA
FSHW011959200619
59279FS